THE CONVERSION OF A KLANSMAN

THOMAS A. TARRANTS III

The Conversion of a Klansman

The Story of a Former Ku Klux Klan Terrorist

A DOUBLEDAY-GALILEE ORIGINAL

DOUBLEDAY & COMPANY, INC., GARDEN CITY, NEW YORK
1979

Grateful acknowledgment is made by the author for permission to quote from the following sources:

"Robert Shelton's Homecoming Address," *The Fiery Cross,* January 1970; *Suicide of the West* by James Burnham, Arlington House, Inc., 1964; *The Unequal Yoke* by Richard V. Pierard, J. B. Lippincott Company, 1971. Copyright © 1971 by Richard V. Pierard. Reprinted by permission of J. B. Lippincott Company.

No copyright is claimed on the material quoted from Federal Bureau of Investigation files.

ISBN: 0-385-14926-3
Library of Congress Catalog Card Number 78-74713
Copyright © 1979 by Thomas A. Tarrants III
All Rights Reserved
Printed in the United States of America
First Edition

FOREWORD

It was a hot spring day in the Delta country of Mississippi. The chaplains at the Mississippi State Penitentiary at Parchman had invited me to conduct a service for the prison population. As the meeting began, I was somewhat nervous, for I was to speak from a makeshift platform in the center of the rodeo ring, a long distance from the stands. Eye contact would be difficult. The prisoners sat spaced far apart from each other in clusters. Some were restless, a few openly hostile. Many of the men seemed interested only in eyeing the female prisoners seated on the opposite side of the ring.

Two impressions remain with me from that day. I remember feeling unusual liberty as I spoke, and that the audience did listen attentively. But my most lasting impression was of a prisoner I met. One of the chaplains had especially wanted me to speak to him, for he told me that this young man had a strong Christian witness within the prison.

After the service we talked briefly. Physically, I recall only that he was tall. But the overwhelming sense left with me was that of a human being who was intelligent, warm, gentle, and who was filled with a love for God and people.

That is how I first met Tommy Tarrants.

Later, when I learned his story and then read in this book the details, I could scarcely put the two together. Was it possible that the gentle man I met in prison could be the violent man I read of in this book?

The answer is both yes and no. It is the same Tommy Tarrants—but a new man, a man transformed by the greatest miracle of them all—the life-renewing grace of God.

This is an important book. It is more than just another conversion story. It is significant because it magnifies the grace of a sovereign God. Too often today evangelism is identified with a certain technique or method, as if the correct formula would give us a tool to convert the world. But only the sovereign God could have spared Tommy's life, broken through the stubborn dark ideology that gripped his mind, pierced the barriers of hate, and flooded him with love.

This is a book that also underlines the power of the Bible as the word of God. In a day when some Christians battle over the authority of Scripture, and critics of the Bible scoff at it as an archaic literary fabrication, this book shows that the Bible which spoke so powerfully to Tommy in his prison solitude is still God's hammer to break the proud heart, his light to scatter darkness.

I find in this book also a warning about the danger of religiosity without true salvation. Tommy Tarrants professed faith in Christ, was baptized, and joined a church when he was a young lad. During the years of his most ferocious Klan activities, he imagined he was doing God's will, holding back the hordes of communism. If anyone had suggested he was not en route to heaven, he would have been surprised. It was not until he faced the fact that evil and sin were within his own heart and he needed to be cleansed and changed that he discovered the true meaning of being a child of God. Today when a new wave of religiosity is cresting in America—with an alleged

third of American adults claiming to be "born again"—we
need this clear reminder that a religious experience is not
enough. Faith in Christ, leading to repentance and a
changed life-style, marked by love, joy, and peace, is essential.

THE CONVERSION OF A KLANSMAN is also a sober warning not to identify any one political ideology with the
kingdom of God. Tommy Tarrants unmasks here the psy-
chology—indeed the virulent demonic powers—that lie behind radical movements to the left and right. But all of us
can fall easily into the trap of mistaking our own political
preferences for God's will. This book warns us not to close
our minds to the facts and to be wary of the pride, ego,
and concern for our own well-being that can control our
social and political opinions more than God's word does.

Above all, we have here a powerful reminder that no
human being is beyond the reach of God's grace. As I
have read the story, I have wondered—if I had known
Tommy Tarrants before his Christian conversion, would I
have thought: no use talking to him about Christ—he's
too far gone.

It strikes me that someone may read this book who is
also a prisoner—if not behind stone walls, then locked in
by hate, fear, jealousy, lust, alcohol, drugs, resentment, or
pride. If so, then this book is especially addressed to that
person. At first, Tommy Tarrants was reluctant to publish
his story. He told me that he shrank back from seeming to
be a sensation or publicity seeker. But I reminded him
that the Apostle Paul gave his own testimony again and
again of how God changed him from a persecutor of the
church to an apostle of love.

A final word on behalf of Tommy Tarrants. Pray for
this young man. With the publication of this book, he will
be subject to intense publicity. The media will latch on to
him. Some thoughtless religious groups may even try to
exploit him. Radical groups may oppose him. Skeptics

may scoff at him. As I have grown to know Tommy as a friend, I know that he does not relish being in the spotlight; his own preference would be to study and teach God's word in some quiet place. So pray that his roots may grow deep in God, that he will keep humble, growing, and teachable, that brothers and sisters may surround him with a network of prayer and support.

Pray above all that as his story is read by thousands there may come a new realization that the body of Christ has in the cross of Christ a source of love to change the world that will outlast the twisted cross of the Klan.

Leighton Ford
Charlotte, North Carolina
February 1979

PROLOGUE

I was in prison. The press and the radio people had described me as the most dangerous man in Mississippi. I had been placing bombs for the Ku Klux Klan and I had shot a state trooper. They had sentenced me to thirty years. I had escaped, but they caught me and now I was in the maximum security unit. It was there that I began reading the Bible again. I can't really say why. Whatever the reason, I started reading in the New Testament, and as I did, the experience was extraordinary. For one thing, I wasn't bored as I always had been. But more important, I was able to understand clearly what I read. The Bible became an open book—a living Word. Charged with meaning, it spoke directly to me. It was almost as if I had been blind all my life and had just received my sight.

The light that lit up within me opened up a whole new world in the Bible. Now for the first time I realized that I was lost. I had always had a mental knowledge of the Truth, to be sure: I knew that all men were sinners and needed to be saved through acceptance of Christ as Savior. But although I knew these truths intellectually and had even made a verbal profession of faith in Christ in my early teens, I had never had a personal encounter with the living Christ. I had never really felt the weight of my sin. To me it had been a theoretical truth but never personally felt and experienced. Now it became a reality for me. I realized that I had never repented of my sin and surrendered myself to Jesus Christ, living and incarnate. I had merely gone through the forms and said the right words. I had never been "born again."

One verse of Scripture was especially penetrating: "What does it profit a man if he gain the whole world and lose his own soul? And what will a man give in exchange for his soul?" Yes. This was it. For the previous five years I had been selling my soul to gain the world. Although I thought I was motivated by dedication to my ideals, in truth I used my activities to receive recognition, acceptance, and approval from my peers. In other words, my activities provided me with a sense of worth. They fed my ego.

As the full impact of all this began to break upon me, I was overcome with a sense of my sinfulness—not just for prejudice, hatred, and political violence, but for my whole life-style. All my life I had been living for myself—what pleased me, made me feel good, made me look good to others. The feelings, needs, desires of other people were always secondary to what I wanted. Indeed, the whole world revolved around me and this showed itself in the outward sins of my life.

As I came to see myself as I really was—as God saw me —I was crushed, and I wept bitterly. How hideous and wretched I was. Then, seeing my need so clearly and knowing there was only One who could meet it, I surrendered myself to the Lord Jesus Christ as fully as I knew how. A tremendous weight was lifted from me, and I began to feel peace at last.

THE CONVERSION OF A KLANSMAN

CHAPTER ONE

On a hot summer afternoon Kathy Ainsworth and I made the twenty-minute drive from Jackson, Mississippi, to the Ross Barnett Reservoir just north of town. The twenty-seven-mile-long reservoir, surrounded by lush woods, is a popular sporting and recreation area. We were going for supper at The Captain's Table out on the eastern shore, one of the nicer restaurants in the area.

We drove past Main Harbor Marina on the reservoir's southern end and up on the dam, which forms a short stretch of the eastern shore. As the reservoir came into full view, its placid waters reflected the late evening sun, while anglers quietly tested their luck from the shore line.

The road began to veer away from the water's edge, and land was on both sides of us as we reached the upper end of the dam. Presently we turned down a green land-scaped drive that wound through a sprawling, tree-shaded picnic area and back out to the shore line again. Passing another marina, we came to the brow of a small cove, where the road ended in the parking lot of The Captain's Table, and I parked my dark green Buick Electra.

We took a table by a large window overlooking the water. It was a noneventful, quiet Saturday evening as we ate and talked and watched the setting sun cast its reflection across the lake. Little did Kathy and I know that in a few hours the peaceful stillness of this evening would end in a wild police chase and bloody gun battle.

During the previous five years I had become a hardened radical. Starting innocently in the Goldwater for President campaign at the age of sixteen, I soon became involved with members of the John Birch Society. A short time later, I moved into the National States' Rights Party, the Ku Klux Klan, and the Minutemen. For nearly a year, I had headed a small, highly secret, elite terrorist group. I was largely responsible for planning and directing the Ku Klux Klan's terrorist operations against civil rights forces, communists, liberals, and Jews. I was a leader of Mississippi's dreaded White Knights of the Ku Klux Klan, the most violent right-wing organization in the United States. Among its achievements in five years were nine murders and more than three hundred other acts of violence, including bombings, burnings, and beatings.

Kathy was not like this. She wasn't the cold, calculating kind of radical I was. Warm, attractive, and intelligent, she was a schoolteacher who was loved by her students and well respected in the community. To the casual observer and even many of her friends, Kathy seemed to be the typical Mississippian, strongly opposed to integration but content to voice that opposition through organizations that worked within the system.

But Kathy, even from childhood in Miami, had been exposed to the views and influence of right-wing radicals. Several of them were so radical that they had to move away from Miami when they no longer could function effectively. Kathy had long been acquainted with them and their ideology. In fact, I had first met her in 1966 through two of these former Miamians one weekend when she had visited in their new home in Mobile.

About two years later, on that June night in 1968, as we ate steak and seafood, we discussed our plans to bomb the house of Meyer Davidson, a prominent Jewish businessman, later that night in Meridian, Mississippi, a city of some forty thousand.

Several weeks earlier Davidson had spoken out in great indignation after the bombing of Temple Beth Israel, Meridian's Jewish synagogue. Boldly attacking the Ku Klux Klan, he had denounced its members as maniacs and had launched a fund-raising drive to obtain eighty thousand dollars in reward money. This alone would have been sufficient provocation for an attack, but other more practical considerations had also influenced our decision to bomb his house.

During the previous six months, the Klan had maintained a reign of terror in the Meridian area. Since January 15, 1968, eight black churches had been fire-bombed or burned and two black homes, as well as one white home, had been fired into. Two Klansmen, Raymond Roberts and Jerry Rochek, were prime suspects and were under surveillance and investigation by the FBI, state, and local authorities.

They had been able to handle the pressure quite well until the bombing of Temple Beth Israel and Davidson's outcry in the national press. But at that point State Public Safety Commissioner Giles Crisler sent a special squad of state investigators to Meridian to assist local police in harassing the two men. In an effort to cause them either to talk or make a mistake, this special team followed them everywhere they went, watching their homes around the clock, coming to their jobs, and even threatening their lives.

The intensity of the situation soon began to take its toll on Rocheck, and Roberts asked one of my associates for our help. On Thursday, June 13, Raymond came to Jackson to discuss the matter. The next Tuesday, my colleague went to Meridian for further discussions with Raymond and his brother Wayne. As the talks progressed, it was obvious that something had to be done soon to relieve the pressure. It was decided that this could best be accomplished by another major act against Jews that would be consistent with our continuing terror campaign and that would appear to be the work of those who bombed the synagogue. This time, however, it would be done in such a way that it would appear that the prime suspects could not have been involved. Roberts and Rochek would know in advance the time of the bombing and would be in a public place with many witnesses. The police would then reason that because they weren't involved in the second act, they probably weren't involved in the first either. Thus, the focus of the investigation—and harassment—would shift elsewhere.

Although my colleague had handled the discussions and planning up to this point, the choice of Meyer Davidson as the target was not entirely his doing. Shortly after the synagogue bombing, I had gone to the Smokey Mountains of North Carolina to a secret haven for right-wing radicals to wait for things to cool off. Before leaving, I had mentioned to him that Meyer Davidson, because of his outcry in the national press, would be a good target for some future operation. With this in mind, the discussions had gravitated toward Davidson as the primary target. When I returned to the state and was briefed on these developments, I gave my hearty approval.

The designated bombers in the original plan were changed at the last minute. One of the Klansmen was under close FBI surveillance and was a prime suspect whenever a major act of violence occurred in central Mississippi. To avoid compromising our operations and to relieve some of the pressure on him, I suggested that he not go on this mission. In that way he would be at home when the bomb exploded and could greet the FBI when agents came knocking on his door minutes later.

I went to Kathy's house and explained the situation.

She was a dedicated right-winger and a trusted member of the Klan inner circle in Jackson. She was also very competent in intelligence gathering, clandestine operations, and the use of firearms. More important, she was a valuable member of our terrorist group and had been involved in previous bombings.

When I arrived at her house, she was preparing to leave for a vacation in Miami, Florida. After discussing the Davidson project, we decided that I would drive her to Miami via Meridian. In this way we could deliver the bomb and then drive on to Florida where she could introduce me to some of her right-wing contacts.

It was extremely humid as we left The Captain's Table and drove to Meridian. But the pleasant atmosphere, excellent cuisine, and beautiful sunset had combined to give us a very nice evening. During the two-hour drive I assured Kathy that it would be a routine operation, just as smooth as our last project together. When the bomb was detonated at 2 P.M., we would be well on our way to Mobile, where she would spend the night with rightist friends before continuing on to Miami.

Bombings are probably the safest and easiest of all terrorist activities. If the bomb is properly designed, it destroys itself, leaving no traceable evidence. And if it is properly delivered, the bomber is seen by no one. Moreover, with such a large number of "high attractiveness–low risk" targets, stakeouts are unlikely under ordinary circumstances.

In the past I had carefully observed certain precautions that had always produced flawless success in bombing missions. The most important was secrecy; information was dispersed on a need-to-know basis. Persons not involved in an operation were not informed of it. However, this time exceptions had been made. Raymond Roberts and his brother Wayne knew the details of the operation but would not be present. But they could be trusted.

They were active terrorists. In fact, Wayne was one of those convicted of killing the three civil rights workers in Philadelphia, Mississippi, in 1964. If anyone could be trusted, it was these two—or so we thought.

Kathy and I reached Meridian about 11 P.M. We stopped at a pay phone near a hamburger stand on the highway, and I called Raymond. Only a few words were spoken, a code signaling him to meet us at a prearranged rendezvous point. In order to circumvent the FBI wiretaps on our phones, we routinely used codes, veiled references, voice disguises, and short calls.

After the call, Kathy and I drove to the rendezvous point—a truck stop several miles east of town where we waited as inconspicuously as possible in the parking area. Within a few minutes Raymond drove up in his white 1965 Chevrolet. He came over to our car and got in the back seat expecting to see me and another Klansman. He was disturbed and surprised at Kathy's presence, but I assured him that she was a competent and trustworthy Klanswoman and that she had been on missions like this before. After talking a few minutes more, Raymond returned to his car and drove to the Holiday Inn where he parked. We followed him, and he got in with us to reconnoiter Davidson's house.

It was a comfortable, brick structure on a spacious, tree-shaded corner lot. We circled the block twice and drove through the immediate neighborhood, looking for anything suspicious that might indicate surveillance or a stakeout. The streets were quiet and dark except for an occasional streetlight, and no one was out. It looked perfect.

After the reconnaissance, we took Raymond back to the Holiday Inn. When the bomb exploded, he would have been in the bar for two hours and would have an airtight alibi.

Then we drove to a wooded area several miles north of

town on U. S. Highway 45. Here I took the bomb from the trunk of the car, checked out the electrical circuitry, set the timer for 2 A.M., then put it on the front seat between Kathy and me. This bomb was different from those I had used previously. In the past I had always built my own bombs, using conventional dynamite, detonator cap, and fuse. These were simple to construct, safe and easy to use, and virtually impossible to trace. This bomb, however, had an electrical detonator, activated by a mercury switch and clock and wired into twenty-nine sticks of dynamite.

We now returned to the city. As we turned south down Twenty-ninth Street, the dim light of a distant streetlight brought Davidson's house into view. It was almost 1 A.M. now, and neighbors were asleep. We slowed to a stop about fifty feet in front of the drive leading to the carport of Davidson's house. The house was about forty feet from the street. On our left, directly across the street from Davidson's was a five-foot embankment with trees and shrubbery that partially hid a house from view.

A certain stillness pervaded the warm, humid night, as I quietly opened the car door and stepped out in the street. Kathy remained in the car. Tucking a 9-mm Browning automatic pistol into the waistband of my trousers, I took the bomb from the front seat, closed the car door, and calmly walked around the front of my car and into Davidson's yard. I was on the driveway, heading toward the carport. Soon this mission would be completed like so many others in the past, and Kathy and I would be on our way to Miami.

Suddenly a shot rang out in the dark. Then possibly a shout. Then more shots in rapid succession. Instantly I dropped the bomb and spun around to head for the car, and my pistol fell to the ground unfired. A thousand thoughts raced through my mind as I ran. . . . Davidson must have seen us and fired warning shots. . . . Where were the shots coming from? . . . Now I had to reach the car and clear the area before police came.

As I reached the front of the car, I was hit in the upper right leg with a full load of buckshot fired from close range. Where could it be coming from? The embankment? Yes, the embankment. Marksmen were concealed in the bushes on the embankment just a few yards from the car—and I had been running straight toward them. I staggered, grabbing the left front of the car to keep from falling. Bullets were flying everywhere now, but somehow I made it to the door, and Kathy opened it to help me in. The riflemen were pumping round after round of rifle and shotgun fire into the car. As Kathy helped me in, she was hit. I hurriedly started the engine, floor-boarded the accelerator, and sped away in a hail of gunfire. Warm blood gushed out of my leg onto the seat.

"Tommy, I've been hit," Kathy said in a soft voice. Quickly glancing over at her, I saw a bullet wound at the base of her neck. "I've been hit, too, Kathy," I said. "But we're going to make it. Don't worry."

There was no answer. When I looked again, she was slumped over on the seat.

Out of nowhere a white police cruiser zoomed up behind me as I raced down Twenty-ninth Street. One officer drove, while the other hung out the window firing a shotgun. Suddenly my rear window was blown out by a blast from the shotgun. They were right on my bumper now. In an effort to evade them, I made a fast right turn at the next intersection, then another. But the heavy Buick Electra was no match for the lighter and faster Ford. They stayed right on my bumper, pumping round after round into the car.

In a desperate effort I made another turn, this time to the left. But my front tires had been hit and gave way as I made the turn, causing me to skid up over the curb and come to a rest half in the street and half in the yard of a corner house. The cruiser was so close behind that it couldn't stop, and rammed into my rear. By now I had lost a great deal of blood and was operating on adrenaline.

More reacting than thinking, I grabbed my 9-mm submachine gun from under the front seat, jumped out of the car, and fired a sustained burst into the cruiser. Patrolman Mike Hatcher had jumped from his door at the same time with a shotgun, but I had been faster, and three rounds of machine-gun fire hit him in the chest as I sprayed the front windshield. His partner, who had been driving, ducked beneath the dash and was missed by the burst. My clip had emptied, so I dropped the gun there in the street. The other patrolman stood up and fired a shotgun blast that struck me in the upper left leg and abdomen.

I staggered but managed to keep moving and made my way to some shrubbery in the backyard of a house nearby. More concerned with his wounded partner than with me, the patrolman radioed for help instead of firing again. I tried to scale the fence in the back of the yard, but the top strand was electrically charged and I fell to the ground. By now I had lost a great deal of blood and was nearly in shock. I had no strength to do anything but lie there in the bushes where I fell.

Everything was growing dim. Each heartbeat pushed me a little further out into the darkness, like a boat drifting slowly into a foggy night. Soon, very soon, I would be asleep.

Sirens were coming in from every direction, police cars one after another and ambulances. Officers fanned out with searchlights. Suddenly a beam fell on me.

"Here he is, in the bushes," a voice said.

Four men approached slowly, holding a light on me each step of the way. I lay very still with my eyes closed, lest some movement should cause them to shoot. About ten feet away they stopped and turned off the light. Then there were four deafening blasts in rapid succession. Two ripped into my right arm, nearly tearing it off. The other two hit the ground only inches from my chest.

By now numbness had spread throughout my body and I had very little sensation of pain. I was drifting further and further into blackness but could still hear what was going on around me.

A light was shining on me again and one of the officers said to another, "Is he dead?" Someone began dragging me out of the bushes and said, "No, the son of a bitch is still alive."

Just as they pulled me out onto the grass, someone called for a stretcher, and I was loaded into a waiting ambulance along with Kathy.

CHAPTER TWO

The ambulance driver exchanged a few brief words with the attendant as he turned on the siren and began the drive to Meridian's Mattie Hersey Hospital. It was then that I knew for certain that the gaping wound at the base of Kathy's neck had been fatal.

Death was close now for me too. I felt stunned, and it was difficult for me to concentrate. I was barely conscious, but I still held on.

When we reached the hospital I opened my eyes and, with dimmed vision, could make out police cars and lawmen waiting for me. As the attendant wheeled me into the emergency room, FBI agents, state investigators, highway patrolmen, and city police were everywhere.

Doctors and nurses quickly began to work. My blood-soaked clothes were skillfully cut away with surgical scissors, and I lay naked while probes were inserted carefully into the bullet holes to determine the extent of my injuries. I felt degraded—captured and helpless while my enemies looked upon me with contempt. I was defeated and confused. I couldn't understand how all this had happened. It was like a fuzzy scene from a dream.

I asked for a painkiller but couldn't have any because I was so close to death. My mouth, tongue, and throat were dry. Water . . . I asked for water. But I couldn't have any.

At last small shavings of ice were placed on my tongue, and the relief was incredibly pleasant—even in the midst of pain.

When I had been wheeled into the emergency room, the doctor gave me a maximum of forty-five minutes to live. So as the doctors frantically worked to prepare me for surgery, lawmen tried to secure a deathbed confession. Their prime interest was to link Sam Bowers, Imperial Wizard of the White Knights of the Ku Klux Klan, and Danny Hawkins, my closest associate, to the bombing, but true to the Klan's Code of Secrecy, I told them nothing.

I was then wheeled into a dingy, old-fashioned operating room where a bright overhead light shone directly into my eyes. Nurses scurried around getting me ready for surgery and administered an anesthetic. Within seconds I was unconscious.

Later that morning in Mobile, the phone rang at the apartment of my girl friend. The Meridian police had found her phone number in my wallet and were calling to notify her of what had happened. She immediately called my mother who picked her up within minutes and drove to my grandmother's house where my father lived.

When my father heard the news from my mother and grandmother, he was distraught. Once he had recovered from the shock, however, they all got in the car and drove to Meridian, 140 miles away.

My girl friend was a petite, attractive brunette, and we had been close for many months. I loved her very much, and so did my family—especially Mother. At one point prior to my going underground we had almost decided to marry. And the night I left she had sobbed and pleaded with me not to go. Now her worst fears were confirmed.

Later I was to learn that someone had telephoned my grandmother around four-thirty on the afternoon before I was captured. He asked to speak to Thomas Tarrants III.

My grandmother told him I wasn't there and that she didn't know where I was. He said he had to get in touch with me "right away."

The caller then asked if I had gone to Mississippi. My grandmother said she didn't know but that she would "give anything in this world to know." Then he said again, "I've got to get him right away." As I now think back about that call, I have no doubt that someone was trying to warn me of the situation in Meridian.

I had been unconscious since going into surgery at about two-thirty that Sunday morning. Slowly, almost imperceptibly, I began to regain consciousness. An IV needle was uncomfortably lodged in my left arm, and I could now hear the nurses moving about the room, monitoring my vital signs and checking circulation in my wounded arm.

I slowly opened my eyes as best I could—still heavily sedated. The room was old.

In what seemed like only a few moments my mother, father, and girl friend entered the room. Lovingly they assured me that they would stand by me and that I would receive the best possible medical treatment. It felt so good to see them and to be with those who loved me— even if only for a minute or two.

Outside the door it was an armed camp, with heavily armed state and local law-enforcement officers. Few, if any, cared whether I lived or died, and many preferred the latter.

My arm had been severely mangled by the shotgun blasts. After the surgeons had cleaned out the wound, removing the bone splinters and fragments, they found that a four-inch section of the ulna bone just below the elbow had been shot away. It was a very difficult case, and amputation was being strongly considered. There was, however, a slight chance of saving my arm, but it would require the skill of an exceptional specialist in orthopedic surgery.

Ironically, Meridian was the home of one of the best orthopedic surgeons in the United States, Dr. Leslie Rush, who headed Rush Memorial Hospital in Meridian. Dr. Rush had pioneered in the use of stainless-steel pins and screws for bone surgery. My family talked to him about my situation, and after examining me, he volunteered to operate without charge.

Arrangements were made for my transfer to Rush Memorial Hospital, and on July 3, 1968, three days after my capture, I was taken in a large, heavily armed police convoy from Mattie Hersey to an operating suite at Rush Hospital. Rush was a bright, clean, modern hospital, and I was relieved to be there. Upon arrival I was x-rayed, then taken directly into surgery. Police were everywhere: outside the hospital, at every entrance, inside the building, and even in the operating room during surgery.

When I awoke from surgery hours later, an IV drip flowed into my left arm and my right arm throbbed with intense, sharp pain. A policeman who was sitting in the room guarding me called the nurses and I was given a shot that quickly returned me to a painless and peaceful unconsciousness. This was to be the first of many such shots, which would come at four-hour intervals throughout the next few weeks.

The facilities here were much better than at Mattie Hersey. I was in a nice modern room in an area of the hospital that had been placed off limits to all but a few carefully chosen doctors and nurses. Police officers sat in my room around the clock, and in the hall outside. Several were always in the room across the hall. Still others guarded the entrances to the hospital and patrolled surrounding streets. They were taking no chances.

The primary reason for such heavy security was the fear that the Klan might try either to rescue or to liquidate me. Law-enforcement officials were aware of my extensive contacts among paramilitary-oriented rightists. Some of these people would not shrink from a daring commando-type rescue operation if it was feasible. In early spring, I had been in California conferring with the West Coast coordinator of the Minutemen, a paramilitary underground organization. The leader of the organization and his chief aide were even then being sought by federal agents. FBI intelligence indicated that the two might be headed to Mississippi to assist me if possible. But there was another concern. I knew enough about Klan operations to put away permanently the top leadership of the KKK in Mississippi and certain key radicals elsewhere; so my liquidation would preclude any information being extracted from me, either willingly or unwillingly. One of my Klan friends did, in fact, suggest a plan to poison me, but it apparently was never seriously considered. When I learned of the plan I was not offended because we regarded everyone as expendable for the cause.

The only visitors I could have were members of my immediate family. My father, mother, brother, and sister came to see me as often as police would permit—almost daily at first. My grandmother and my girl friend, who faithfully accompanied my family on the many trips, were made to wait downstairs and never got to see me.

For the first few days at Rush I was fed intravenously and kept heavily sedated. Every four hours I was given a shot of Demerol, a potent painkiller with euphoric effects. Gradually, however, I developed a tolerance to it, which meant that increasingly larger or more frequent injections would be necessary for the same effect. But such increases would result in addiction. So I had to suffer. There was no other alternative. And for more than two weeks I endured excruciating pain.

This would have been bad enough by itself, but the very awkward and uncomfortable position in which I had to lie seemed to make the pain more acute. Because of the nature of my wound and the program of treatment, I had to lie on my back with my right arm positioned in an upward incline. Then, I always had to keep my hand and forearm resting on pillows in an elevated position. So I was on my back almost constantly, which made sleeping— even resting—difficult. Changing positions, which was necessary on occasion, was a painful ordeal. My nights were agonizing periods of intermittent sleep and intense pain.

Nonetheless, my condition stabilized, the IV drips were discontinued, and I began eating solid food again. I quickly learned to write and eat with my left hand. Until then it had never occurred to me that I would have so much appreciation for such a simple pleasure as eating. I continued to gain strength with each passing day, and my nurses were soon walking me around the room and down the hall—even though I had been wounded in both legs. The danger of blood clots or pneumonia far outweighed the risk of my getting up and walking a little each day.

Good doctors and good facilities certainly played a large part in my survival and recovery from a human standpoint. But another, less obvious factor was the encouragement and support of my family and the kindness and compassion of Dr. Rush and the nurses who cared for me. These people were a welcome relief from the policemen around me, many of whom were cold, hard, and bitter.

I had been at Rush about ten days when a surprising exception was made to the no-visitor policy. One afternoon Percy Quinn, an attorney from Laurel, Mississippi, was permitted to see me. He had been sent by Sam Bowers to see firsthand how I was doing, learn the details of the ambush, and reassure me of Klan support. Quinn was not the most sought-after of the Klan's lawyers and was no doubt sent because the situation was so hopeless.

He was supposed to represent me and try to arrange bond, but he confided to my family that there was nothing he could do to help me.

A few days later I was scheduled for more surgery. Early that morning a nurse gave me a shot, and a few minutes later two orderlies came in and placed me on a cart. At least half a dozen policemen with submachine guns and sawed-off shotguns surrounded me as they wheeled the cart to the elevator and down to the operating suite. I could never decide if they were afraid I was going to jump up and run away or if they expected someone to sweep me up in his arms and dash out of the hospital. In any case, when we reached the operating room where a number of other officers were waiting, my escorts seemed noticeably relieved.

The surgery went well, and in a couple of days I was back in the same routine. Then one morning a couple of new nurses came to my room. They were physiotherapists and had come to teach me how to exercise my fingers to prevent them from becoming stiff from nonuse. From then on I flexed and exercised my fingers several times a day. Gradually I regained near-normal use of my hand after the arm wound healed.

During those long days and nights I can remember reading from a volume of the New Testament that had been placed in the room by the Gideons. I was looking for hope, inspiration, and encouragement. But like many times in the past when I had read the Bible (to support racist ideology), it was a rather dull, tedious book that I found difficult to read. So I gave it up and concentrated on another matter that had bothered me ever since the ambush.

How had the FBI and police known our plan? Unlike all other Klan groups, our unit operated in a well-organized, sophisticated, almost professional way. We observed the strictest security precautions. What had gone wrong? As I lay there in bed day after day, many times with my eyes closed, I often caught snatches of conversation between the policemen guarding me. On several occasions officers casually discussed the incident with me. On the basis of things they said and questions they asked, it soon became obvious that they had considerable inside information. In various ways and with varying degrees of subtlety, they tried to pick information from me, but they only succeeded in giving me a general idea of what they already knew.

During my last week in the hospital I had an unexpected visitor—Mike Hatcher, the police officer I had wounded in the shoot-out when I was captured. Although he had been hit three times in the chest (once in the heart) and had undergone open-heart surgery, he looked healthy and well. I didn't recognize him until he introduced himself and shook my hand. Then it became a rather awkward situation. I didn't know what to say, so I asked how he was doing. He said that he was fine and told me that he just wanted to let me know that he was a better man than I was. Exactly what he meant I didn't know. Perhaps he was referring to his stamina in surviving a more serious wound than mine and to the fact that he recovered before I did. Or maybe he was alluding to the fact that the police had finally won. Although the exchange between us was understandably cool, there was no outward hostility, and he soon left.

Later that year, he sent a Christmas card to my parents bearing the handwritten note, "Only God can take care of his lost sheep." Little did he—or they—know how prophetic those words were.

Finally, on August 2, after a month of hospitalization, I was well enough to be transferred to the Lauderdale County Jail to await trial. About midmorning, Sheriff Alton Allen came to my room and told me to get ready to leave. Until now I had been in a clean, modern hospital where conditions were good and people pleasant. The thought of going to a dirty, dismal jail for months of solitary isolation was very depressing, but I showed no sign of emotion. Half an hour later, in pajamas and robe, I was taken by wheelchair to the emergency room where the sheriff and his deputies helped me into a car for the short ride to the jail.

CHAPTER THREE

In less than five minutes we pulled up in front of the courthouse, a large, gray stone building five stories tall that covered an entire block in downtown Meridian. The police sealed off all traffic on the street while I slowly limped into the building with heavy escort. Policemen and highway patrolmen armed with shotguns and scoped high-powered rifles at the ready, stood in front of the courthouse and in the street as well.

Once inside the building, I was taken by elevator to the fourth floor, where the jail was. Here I was met by the jailor, a tall, gray-haired man named Buck Lewis. He led the way to the cell I was to occupy. It actually was an entire cellblock, vacated and reserved exclusively for me. Here I would spend the next four and one-half months alone, seeing and talking with no one but the jailor and, on visiting days, my parents.

We entered the cellblock through a heavy steel door that opened into a room about twenty feet wide and thirty feet long. The walls were solid concrete except for two or three windows through which one could see several buildings, including the Lamar Hotel just across the street. In the middle of this room, running lengthwise, was a rectangular steel dining table and in the near left corner was a small shower stall without a curtain. Along the full length of the right wall were four, four-man cells with sliding doors that opened into the day room. These cells were very small—perhaps seven by ten feet. In addition to the four bunks, stacked two high on either side of the cell, there was a face bowl and commode just inside each cell door.

I was directed to the first cell, and the sliding door clanked shut behind me. I was given two clean sheets to cover the old, dirty mattress that was in the cell, and then everyone left.

Until this point I had been in an antiseptic environment with people around me all the time. But with the clanging of the door, all that had changed. I was all alone now in a dimly lit, dirty jail surrounded by concrete and steel. I could feel nothing but despair. Trapped in this cell, I felt utterly defeated and saw no hope for the future. Certainly this was the lowest moment of my life. Indeed, my whole life was shattered, and the full impact of it came crashing down on me with the closing of that cell door. There's no way to describe the total aloneness that I felt.

The stark reality of my predicament was more than I could bear, and for the first time since my arrest, I broke down and began to cry. For a long time I wept uncontrollably. For five years my whole life had centered on "the cause." I had given myself to it with passionate devotion, just as a man gives himself to his wife or his God. Indeed, for me it was a god.

The depth and intensity of this commitment is hard for the average person to understand. Perhaps the best expression of it is reflected in a letter written by an American communist breaking his engagement with his fiancée. He speaks for all radicals, right or left, when he says:

> We communists suffer many casualties. We are those whom they shoot, hang, lynch, tar and

feather, imprison, slander, fire from our jobs and whose lives people make miserable in every way possible. Some of us are killed and imprisoned. We live in poverty. From what we earn we turn over to the Party every cent which we do not absolutely need to live.

We communists have neither time nor money to go to movies very often, nor for concerts nor for beautiful homes and new cars. They call us fanatics. We are fanatics. Our lives are dominated by one supreme factor—the struggle for world communism. We communists have a philosophy of life that money could not buy.

We have a cause to fight for, a specific goal in life. We lose our insignificant identities in the great river of humanity; and if our personal lives seem hard, or if our egos seem bruised through subordination to the Party, we are amply rewarded—in the thought that all of us, even though it be in a very small way, are contributing something new and better for humanity.

There is one thing about which I am completely in earnest—the communist cause. It is my life, my business, my religion, my hobby, my sweetheart, my wife, my mistress, my meat and drink. I work at it by day and dream of it by night. Its control over me grows greater with the passage of time. Therefore I cannot have a friend, a lover or even a conversation without relating them to this power that animates and controls my life. I measure people, books, ideas and deeds according to the way they affect the communist cause and by their attitude to it. I have already been in jail for my ideas, and if need be, I am ready to face death.

This is how I felt about the radical Right, but now, as I sat locked in this cell, I could no longer pursue this holy cause. It would fall to others to carry on the work while I sat languishing in prison. In a word, my purpose in life had been to advance the cause and now that that was no longer possible, my reason for existence had vanished.

During the first few days in jail I was extremely depressed and probably would have committed suicide had it been possible. For me life had come to an end; there was no point in continuing. Dying would have been easier than living and much more preferable.

Coping with life under these circumstances was difficult, to say the least. For a time I read the Bible, as many people do during times of adversity. But, in any event, halfway through the Old Testament I became bored and laid it aside. What I hoped to find in it I'm not quite sure—perhaps some sort of comfort or consolation. In a sense I guess I was trying to use it as a crutch.

My other coping mechanism was sleep. I slept as much as possible because I didn't have to face my problems while I was asleep. Between reading and sleeping, I was able to keep my mind largely off my problems. Or to put it another way, I was able to escape.

Daily jail life was routine. Breakfast was served around 6 A.M. and consisted of grits, biscuits, syrup, fried bologna, and an egg. Later in the morning, Mr. Lewis brought a couple of black trusties who swept and mopped the cellblock. Lunch was the best meal of the day, good home-cooked southern food and corn bread. Snacks and sodas were also available at a reasonable price.

On Wednesdays and Sundays visitors were allowed. I really looked forward to those days because my mom and dad drove from Mobile each visiting day to spend time with me and bring snacks and reading material. Apricot juice, cashews, and fig bars were my favorite foodstuffs, and periodicals such as *Time, Newsweek, U.S. News and*

World Report, and the *National Observer* provided me
with hours of reading enjoyment.

For four months (until I was tried and sentenced to
prison) my parents visited me faithfully in the Lauderdale County Jail, coming at least once a week and often
twice. It was quite a strain on them to make the 145-mile
trip to Meridian so frequently, but they never com-
plained. To me this is especially remarkable because I
was an extremely self-centered person and showed little
consideration for them. I was generally short-tempered,
irritable, and moody, being preoccupied with my predicament. Hard, cold, unfeeling, and pessimistic, I was, for the
most part, insensitive to what my parents were going
through and had gone through. Their heartaches and
agonies were beyond my comprehension and of little concern to me.

How had I become so callous? I hadn't always been.
But my total commitment to the cause changed my life.
Once I had firmly embraced radical ideology, I began to
develop an obsession and hatred. These two factors produced a reorientation of my value system and attitudes.
The cause became a holy cause and thus assumed the
status of a god. When I reached this point, I began to
make decisions only on the basis of what would advance
the cause. The end justified the means. The ruthlessness
that ensues from such an attitude hardens a person emo-
tionally and renders him increasingly more calloused and
unfeeling. If indulged in long enough, this moral insanity
ultimately produces what can only be described as pys-
chotic radicalism. This was my condition.

Several weeks after my transfer to the jail two FBI
agents came to visit me. Frank Watts and Jack Rucker
were warm, personable men, and for some reason I liked
them—even though I now hated the FBI. Their visit, of
course, came as no surprise. They knew that I was in a
position to supply a great deal of vital information about

important rightist leaders, their groups, and activities. I could give testimony that would put some in prison for a long time. Moreover, I could help them solve a number of cases they could not break. Thus, I knew it was only a matter of time until they would try to see if I could be persuaded to co-operate with the Bureau. From the very beginning, then, I knew what their ultimate objective was, and they knew I knew. Nonetheless, because I agreed to talk with them, they thought that negotiation was at least a possibility.

The truth is, however, that I had no intention whatever of co-operating with them in any way. I agreed to talk with them because I liked them and enjoyed matching wits.

During the course of our talks, Frank realized how warped my views of God were and asked his pastor, Dr. Bev Tenin of First Baptist Church in Meridian, to come visit me. Frank had developed a real concern for my spiritual condition, but I saw nothing wrong with myself and was, of course, suspicious of Dr. Tenin's motives. So I gained nothing from talking with him.

As the date of my trial approached, my parents began pressing me to co-operate with the attorneys they had engaged. Thomas Haas, a former assistant U.S. attorney from Mobile, was our family lawyer and was retained by the family to represent me. This was very objectionable to me. I had a strong dislike for Tom because of what I considered to be an entirely too moderate position on race and civil rights issues. Without doubt he was a fine attorney, but I simply didn't like him and didn't trust him. The other attorney, Roy Pitts of Meridian, also was capable, although less experienced. But for some reason I liked and trusted him.

Haas, a specialist in constitutional law, had decided that my only defense was insanity. His sincere belief was that anyone with views like mine had to be crazy. But under the existing law—the McNaughton Law—I was not legally insane because I knew all too well the difference between right and wrong at the time of the crime. Decrying this sad state of affairs and convinced that radicals like me were insane, Haas decided to attempt to challenge and overthrow the McNaughton Law, using me as the test case.

I was infuriated with this strategy—especially because he actually believed that I was insane. This was a gross personal affront and an appalling insult to the cause that I had served with such dedication. His assertions were in line with the rather common contention among our enemies in the liberal camp that rightist radicals were sick—mentally ill. So to consent to such a defense was playing into the hands of our enemies and making a mockery of all I believed in and had fought for so hard and so long.

Thus, I adamantly refused to co-operate with Haas or even consider his plan. In fact, I insisted that he be fired. But my parents would hear nothing of this and continued to press for my co-operation. The impasse was broken when my girl friend pled with me to co-operate. For some reason, her appeals moved me when no others could, and I gave in.

Haas immediately called in one of the leading psychiatrists in the Southeast, Dr. Claude Brown. After talking with the family, Dr. Brown came to Meridian and talked with me in the jail for about forty-five minutes.

The trial was scheduled for November, but even before it began, Haas was busy filing motions and carefully laying out traps for the court and prosecution. Later he would use them to appeal the decision. The trial itself proceeded smoothly, with the prosecution presenting eye witnesses (police officers) to the bombing attempt and Haas presenting Dr. Brown as the key defense witness. After my mother testified about the marked changes in my attitudes, values, and behavior when I joined the rightist movement, Dr. Brown took the stand. He testified that in his opinion I was insane and should be given psychiatric treatment rather than sent to prison. In rebuttal, the prosecution called Dr. Reginald White, director of the East Mississippi State Mental Hospital. After reading Dr. Brown's report, he concluded that I was not insane. Later, during the appeals process, this testimony was confirmed when a team of psychiatrists tested and examined me in great detail and reported to the court that I was "without psychosis, and was functioning at a superior level of intelligence."

The case then went to the jury, which after less than an hour's deliberation rejected the insanity plea and found me guilty of the charge of placing a bomb near a residence.

Judge Lester Williamson then sentenced me to thirty years in the state penitentiary.

Though it may have seemed like a harsh sentence to others, I was relieved it wasn't worse. A life sentence, for example, could never be completely served. It would always be hanging over one's head—even after parole. A thirty-year term, on the other hand, could be served in seventeen years—not counting extra time off for good behavior, which would reduce it even further.

I was then returned to my cell in the jail upstairs. Now, at last, there would be no more suspense. I lay on my cell bunk and breathed several deep breaths. Gradually the tensions of the previous months seemed to roll off of me, and soon I was sound asleep.

CHAPTER FOUR

The predicament I now faced and the life-style that brought me to it were a striking contrast to my earlier life. I had come from a good family. My ancestors had arrived in America from Scotland in 1715 and settled in Jamestown, Virginia. Hard-working, industrious Scotch Presbyterians, they were respectable people who contributed to the building of this nation—leaving the family name in such places as Tarrant County, Texas (Fort Worth), Tarrant City, Alabama (Birmingham), and elsewhere. Later, the name of Daniel Webster was to be one of the most distinguished in the family tree. For many years my grandfather had been a U.S. customs officer. Although Mom's family came to the United States from Scotland later than Dad's, my great-grandmother could remember the Union Army raiding the family plantation during the Civil War. The retelling of such events contributed to the shaping of my values and attitudes.

My paternal grandmother was a strong but loving person who was very firm in her Christian beliefs and seldom missed church. She was of the "old school" and had quite an appreciation for family history and culture—especially southern culture—which she passed on to me. A member of the Daughters of the Confederacy, she was a lover of the Old South and was interested in the Civil War in which her grandfather served as a cavalry colonel. Some of my most enjoyable childhood memories are of those rare occasions when she would talk of the old days and of what life was like when she was growing up in the beautiful bluegrass country of Kentucky.

During the summer of my twelfth year, my grandmother took me to New Orleans for vacation. We stayed at the famous Monteleone Hotel in the French Quarter and hired a horse-drawn carriage and driver to tour the area and explore the shops, galleries, and museums. Restaurants, such as Glucks, were also high-priority spots, although an old graveyard may have been the most fascinating site to me. It rained so hard on our last day in New Orleans that parts of the city were flooded, and I was eager to get back home.

Grandmother, who was financially secure, had a large beautiful house furnished with many elegant antiques. Often I would spend weekends with her. On occasion my brother and sister would also. All the grandchildren loved to stay with her.

I stayed more than the others, however, and was one of her favorites. In fact, I sometimes spent weeks of my summer vacation with her. During such visits I became good friends with the family that lived next door to her. They were of Greek origin and owned a real estate business and restaurants. Their son and I became good friends and spent a lot of time together playing chess, building model boats and planes, and going places. I was almost a part of their family and a number of times I attended services with them at the Greek Orthodox Church.

My parents were good people and reared me well. I can remember how Mom and Dad would take us kids to church. Later Dad quit going—largely because he perceived hypocrisy in church members and because they forced the minister, a fine Christian man, to leave. Having been in business for a while, Dad also knew the reputations of some of these same "church leaders"—which only made matters worse. Gradually only Mother took us to church, and sometimes she sent us and remained home.

My dad worked in auto sales and management. He was a hard worker and had a definite idea of what was right and wrong. Quite frequently he would be at work until 7 or 8 P.M. People liked to do business with him because Dad was honest and truthful in his dealings. As manager of the foreign car department of a large Buick dealership, he was very much troubled by the difficulty of getting parts and service for the cars his department sold. In those days, Jaguars, Triumphs, Renaults, and Opels were not as common as now, and parts were a problem—even if one had a good serviceman. Because of this and other problems, he eventually took a position with another firm. He just felt that he could no longer provide his customers with the kind of deal he would want if he were the customer. This was typical of the strength of his convictions.

A solid family heritage and parents of high ethical standards did not insure harmonious family relationships. My younger brother and sister and I did not get along well. We seemed to fight constantly. I was nice to them as long as they did what I wanted, but when they crossed me I tried to force my will on them, and fights ensued. Sometimes we would join together in a temporary pact to achieve some goal, but once it was achieved, we were back fighting again. On more than one occasion the fights would conclude with me chasing them through the house. Usually we ended up in the dining room, going round and round the table before I caught them. The cause of our disputes often was trivial—such as what TV program to watch—and usually was my fault.

I might feel less uneasy about my family relationships if I had not also been instrumental in some of my parents' disagreements. The sad truth is that I sometimes played them off against each other.

All of their conflicts were not caused by me, but I certainly did not help the situation as my parents' marriage continued to weaken. Eventually Mother and Dad separated, and Dad began to live at Grandmother's. During this time I lived with the parent who gave me the least hassles, and I switched houses several times.

Unquestionably I was a brat. I just couldn't seem to sit still and behave myself. A couple of times I rolled the car out the driveway late at night and went joy riding around town with friends. Another time I bought some liquor for a party to which some friends and I were going. The parents of the girl who was giving the party found the liquor and told my parents. The end result was a good spanking.

Such sheer devilishness and ensuing punishment are overshadowed by the many good memories of my childhood. There were family weekend trips to Florida for swimming and visits to historic sites. One summer Dad and I went to Pensacola for the annual Fiesta of Five Flags Sports Car Races. Numerous times we went to New Orleans to the Audubon Park Zoo, the French Quarter, the museums, and the antique shops.

One of our favorite activities was a day on Dauphin Island—a resort area with beautiful sand dunes and tall pines. Dauphin Island, in the Gulf of Mexico off the Alabama coast, was the site of Fort Gaines, a large Confederate fort that guarded the mouth of Mobile Bay against Union gunboats. My aunt and uncle, who for a time were curators of the fort and its museum, had a large house on the island. Also, another aunt owned some land on the island. So our family often went there for cookouts with friends and relatives.

My misbehavior also was evident in school. Because of the district in which our house was located, I attended Augusta Evans School during the fifth and sixth grades.

Augusta Evans was a good, small public school attended by a number of children from socially prominent families. It was here that my problems really began to intensify. The main reason was my acute consciousness of the socioeconomic gap between myself and the upper-class kids. A number of pupils, in fact a majority, were ordinary middle-class kids like myself. But for some reason I wasn't satisfied with who and what I was. I wanted to be a part of the upper-class group. Although we freely intermingled with little regard for class, I still wanted to be a part of the country-club set. I was friends with most and visited in their homes, and they in mine, but I didn't feel entirely comfortable. To me wealth and status determined one's value. Lacking these, I couldn't feel completely good about myself. Being among the elite and fraternizing with them only made it clearer to me that I was not one of them. I felt that I was inferior.

This problem continued as we moved from one grade to another through junior high school and high school. Indeed, my situation worsened because I projected an attitude of superiority and increasingly sought recognition and acceptance from my peers. Yet the more I sought it, the more I alienated myself from those with whom I wanted to be close. Ironically, the simple truth was that I was accepted and liked from the very beginning. But, not realizing this, I tried to be something I wasn't. As a result I was gradually invited to social functions less and less and tolerated more than accepted.

Because of my discontent, the relationships I did have weren't very deep or satisfying; I missed the type of social interaction that might have corrected my problems. As these needs continued unmet, they intensified and produced frustration.

One can, of course, talk endlessly about complexes, insecurities, and their origins, but in the final analysis their root is pride, which is the essence of sin—and by this curse I was firmly ensnared.

When I was about thirteen I began to worry about what would happen to me if I were to die. Would I go to heaven or hell? The answer was clear. Because I hadn't been "saved," I would go to hell. This fear began to weigh more heavily on my mind, and I began to ask what I needed to do to be saved. My real concern, though, was how to keep from going to hell.

I expressed these fears to my mom and dad, and they called the pastor of our church and asked him to visit me and explain how to be saved. He came over one night and talked with me in the presence of my parents. After reading and explaining some verses of Scripture, he led me in a "prayer of salvation." At the next Sunday night service I was baptized. But neither praying nor the baptism changed me, and my attitude and values were the same. The only difference was that my fear of going to hell was now relieved, and I could enjoy life without this hanging over my head. My ticket to heaven had been punched, and I no longer worried about hell.

But this did not relieve my frustrations. They continued, and by the time I had finished tenth grade I was a simmering cauldron of conflicts and frustration. Trouble wasn't far away.

I found an opportunity to release this frustration a few weeks after school let out between my sophomore and junior years. It was the summer of 1963, and a Republican committee in Washington was circulating petitions urging Senator Barry Goldwater to run for President. My dad, a staunch Democrat, received a letter requesting his support of Goldwater. Although Dad didn't respond, I did. My motivation was largely a dislike for John Kennedy and his policies on race and federal intervention—although I also liked Goldwater's conservatism. It offered a worthwhile cause and a challenge for the summer.

I immediately took the petitions Dad had received and began contacting prominent business and political leaders urging them to sign. After a couple of weeks of meeting and talking with various men, I scheduled a private preorganizational dinner to plan the establishment of the permanent Goldwater for President Committee in Mobile.

When the public meeting occurred on July 30, 1963, these men provided leadership, and I remained in the background, pleased to have had a part in initiating the group.

Present at that public meeting, however, were several members of the John Birch Society who had evidently seen the newspaper announcements of the meeting and wanted to support the Goldwater candidacy. I knew absolutely nothing about the Birchers at that time, but after talking with some of the members and reading their literature, I decided they were good patriotic people.

As I read more and more of their literature and such books as *Masters of Deceit* by J. Edgar Hoover, I became increasingly alarmed about the spread of communism around the world, communist infiltration of the U.S. government, and various communist activities in America. Also, I began to view the U.N. in a new light—as a threat to our national sovereignty. In view of the immediacy of the communist threat to America, the Goldwater campaign diminished in importance to me. After all, if the Birchers were correct—and I thought they were—then we were in danger of a communist takeover very soon. The United States was like a large and beautiful edifice that was being eaten away from within by termites. America might collapse any day.

The impact of this viewpoint really changed my outlook on life. The world was gradually being swallowed up by international communism—Russia in 1917, Eastern Europe in 1946, China in 1947, Cuba in 1959. And the

United States—the only nation strong enough to resist its spread—was itself being undermined from within. Worst of all, most people were unaware or, if they did know, apparently unconcerned.

Being young, impressionable, and idealistic, I saw myself as one of the few who knew of the impending diaster —and therefore one of those reponsible for warning the masses. In other words, a Paul Revere of sorts.

The basic elements of this ideology and my reaction to them have been well summarized by Pierard:

> The unifying factor is an intense, active anti-communism in which life-and-death nature of the struggle overshadows everything else. The Red conspiracy is evident everywhere, and the rightist endeavors to fight it on all fronts. Although the external threat is not completely ignored, the primary emphasis is invariably placed on combatting the domestic enemy, and direct action is the means to victory. A *second* denominator is a full-blown individualism in social, economic, and political relationships. This is reflected in rejection of state-supported welfare programs, advocacy of free enterprise capitalism, and opposition to big government. American patriotism is exalted as the defense against internationalism, which is part of the communist conspiracy. *Third*, a generally negative and pessimistic tone pervades the far right. The victory of the enemy seems almost inevitable because the key decision makers cannot be made aware of the gravity of the Red menace. The rightists have little or no positive program for social advancement which they can offer. A *fourth* characteristic is a common pattern of leadership. Usually heading up rightist groups are such peo-

ple as small-town evangelists, the newly rich, re-
tired military officers, and persons who have
been involved professionally in subversive activities such as former FBI agents, counter-
espionage men, and ex-communists. Also, most
extremists manifest a strong strain of anti-
intellectualism and emphasize emotion rather
than reason. A person need not have any creden-
tials to be an expert on public affairs, and those
who do are frequently looked upon as "egg-
heads." A *sixth* common factor is a tendency toward simplism. People, ideas and events are seen
in stark black-and-white, either-or terms. The
rightist falls back on firm, stereotype views that
permit no ambivalence or half-measures. *Finally,*
such people manifest a deep sense of hostility,
particularly to ideological enemies. They generally feel threatened and alienated and thus direct
hate and aggression toward their foes. This ac-
counts for the unethical and even violent behavior on the part of many ultraconservatives. (*The
Unequal Yoke* by Richard V. Pierard, Lippincott,
1971, pp. 42–44.)

This is a perfect description of how I thought, felt, and
reacted.

About this time acquaintances in the Birchers told me
of a mysterious figure involved in anti-Castro guerrilla activities. During those days there were numerous anti-Castro groups engaged in commando raids on Cuba and
guerrilla warfare. A staunch anticommunist, he had actually been on raids to Cuba himself. He was active in securing support and supplies for such groups in Florida.

Although our relationship was brief, it was significant
because it provided me with my first exposure to the

shadowy and exciting world of clandestine activities and international intrigue.

Because it was sanctioned and covertly supported by the Central Intelligence Agency and because it was anticommunist, I saw it as a patriotic effort to fight communist aggression.

About this same time I heard talk of the Minutemen, a secret paramilitary organization whose purpose was "to be the resistance to and exposure of, the spread of Communist influence within the United States." This involved "the formation of a guerrilla or underground organization." (from FBI files on Thomas Albert Tarrants III.) To this end individuals within the Minutemen (not the organization itself) stockpiled arms, ammunition, and material and were trained in clandestine operations, sabotage, guerrilla tactics, use of weapons, explosives, and so forth—even to the extent of field operations and simulated war games. Moreover, they conducted an intelligence-gathering operation throughout the United States, compiling dossiers on people they considered to be traitors to true Americanism—communists (known and suspected), socialists, and liberals.

As a result of my experiences I developed a lively interest in such subjects as communism, guerrilla warfare and counterinsurgency, sabotage, intelligence work, and clandestine operations. I read countless books on these subjects during the months and years that followed and became well versed in these areas. I also developed a great fondness for firearms and marksmanship, which I studied in such detail that I could identify and operate the military small arms of any nation in the world, and cite their specifications.

Clearly, I was well on my way toward developing expertise in terrorist strategies. I merely needed some practice. The integration of Murphy High School in Mobile provided the first opportunity for such experience.

CHAPTER FIVE

Early in 1963 federal courts had ordered the integration
of Alabama's public schools. Many segregationist rallies
and conferences were called in an effort to mobilize people and plan strategy for resistance. As the opening day of
school drew nearer, tension mounted throughout the
state.

Again and again one heard the charge that communists
controlled the civil rights movement and that integration
would result in interracial marriage, which would weaken
the white race. This would cause the fall of "White Christian Civilization."

When school began on September 4, 1963, I was a very
angry, bitter, and frustrated teen-ager. In addition to my
own unrecognized inner conflicts and tensions, I was furi-
ous at the idea of the federal government forcing my state
and high school to integrate—especially in view of the alleged communist influence in the civil rights movement.
The government seemed to be going right along with
what the communists wanted—a fact that supported what
I had been taught in the summer. Furthermore, southern
values, indeed the whole southern way of life, was under
attack.

I arrived on the huge campus of two thousand students
about half an hour before the two blacks were to arrive

for registration. U.S. marshals and armed National Guard troops were on the scene along with many state troopers and city police. It was an outrage to see such an armed camp. I began talking with students I knew to see what resistance was planned. No one knew of any. I was appalled. I tried to encourage friends and groups to make a protest of some sort, but my efforts were in vain. "What a spineless bunch," I thought in disgust. Later that morning a group of students did demonstrate in protest and a riot ensued, but I had already left and had no part in it.

I was so incensed by the situation that I called Governor George Wallace's office that same day, September 3, to warn him that tension was high and trouble was likely if he didn't take action to block the integration. The FBI learned of this message, and FBI agents called on my dad the next day at his office.

They wanted to know whether he had tried to deliver a message to the director of the Department of Public Safety in Birmingham to the effect that there were twenty-five to thirty U.S. marshals at Murphy High School, that a reception committee was at the school waiting for the arrival of the two black students, and that the situation in Mobile was extremely tense.

My dad suggested that I might possess information along that line. So he brought them to see me. I admitted having called the governor's office, but both my dad and I were very angry about the situation. We were convinced that the FBI had gotten the information by tapping my phone. Because there was such alienation between state and federal officials during this time, we didn't even consider the possibility that the governor's office might be co-operating with the FBI.

After questioning me in detail about the content of my calls to Governor Wallace, the FBI consulted with school officials, and as a result, I was temporarily suspended

from school. Obviously, this generated extreme animosity
in me and my family toward the Bureau.

My suspension lasted only ten days. Then I was back in
school, harassing the two black students and encouraging
others to do the same. This took the form of public in-
sults, name calling, and even hitting and shoving at times.
Had they been boys, it would have been easier to beat
them up, but both were girls, so physical abuse was
limited.

Because I was so frustrated, I tried to get some help
and advice from an outside organization. I contacted the
National States' Rights Party* (NSRP), which was pro-
testing the integration. Founded in 1958, the NSRP had
chapters across the nation and was especially strong in
the South. I first met the leader of the Mobile chapter at
the NSRP headquarters. A tall, impressive man in his late
thirties, he helped me to realize that it was a waste of
time to make Murphy High School a priority in fighting
integration and communism. There were bigger battles to
be fought, battles that would have an infinitely greater

* FBI files on Thomas A. Tarrants III state the following concerning the National States' Rights Party:
On November 26, 1957, a source advised that the United White
Party (UWP) was organized at a convention held in Knoxville,
Tennessee, on November 10, 1957. An article in the November 26,
1957, issue of the *Greenville Piedmont,* a newspaper of Greenville,
South Carolina, reported "the recent formation of a new political
party, to be known as the United White Party." According to the
article, the party was formed at a recently held meeting in Knoxville, Tennessee, at which many Klansmen were represented. The
UWP was reported as being opposed to all "race mixing organizations and individuals."
The July 1958 issue of "The Thunderbolt," self-described as the
"official Racial Nationalist Organ of the National States' Rights
Party" (NSRP), reported that rank and file "States Righters" had
merged with the UWP under "the banner of the National States'
Rights Party," with national offices at Post Office Box 261, Jeffer-
sonville, Indiana.

impact on the situation. As a result, I became active in the NSRP.

I often met with him at his office to discuss at length how the Jews were behind communism and the civil rights movement. Occasionally he would invite me to his house for grilled steaks with him and his wife.

I spent even more time with another NSRP member and a good friend of the organization's leader. He intensively discipled me, meeting me at least once a week and sometimes more. After school was out in the afternoons, he would pick me up, and we would stop at a coffee shop, go to his house, or just drive around. Many times we listened to the sermons and lectures of Dr. Wesley Swift, an anti-Semitic right-wing preacher from California who preached white supremacy. These tapes influenced my beliefs and attitudes toward Jewish people more than anything. And they gave them the authority of religious doctrine.

Through reading books and papers, attending meetings, listening to tapes, and talking with other rightists, my thinking moved even farther to the Right. I became a committed radical rightist. The main difference between the ideology of the far Right and that of the radical Right was largely one of degree and intensity of feeling. Radical rightists believed all the doctrines of far rightists but carried them further. They were obsessed with the threat of domestic subversion and were more inclined to direct action. They bitterly denounced social programs and glorified racial solidarity and patriotism. Emotion rather than reason dictated what was true or false.

Perhaps radical rightists' most distinct characteristic is anti-Semitism. They hold that communism and most of the other ills affecting society are products of an international conspiracy among certain powerful and wealthy Jews, usually international Jewish bankers such as the Rothschilds. Everything is seen in this light. Communism is a Jewish plot to take over the world. In other words, social problems are Jewish-inspired schemes to weaken society. For example, integration is a Jewish plan to destroy the white race through intermarriage with subhuman stock. By a process known as selective perception (accepting only those "facts" that support one's view), radical rightists can present what seems to be a good case to prove their point.

The "Jewishness" of communism, for example, is proven by listing names of Jews who were leaders in the Bolshevik Revolution of 1917 and noting that Karl Marx was from Jewish parents, that Jewish bankers financed the Russian Revolution, and that many Jews held key positions in the Soviet government and in the communist movement.

What isn't mentioned is the fact that Marx's father converted to Christianity when Karl was six years old and that Karl always held Jews in contempt. It is further neglected that the Jewishness of those they cite is merely an accident of ancestry that has had some cultural-ethnic, but no religious influence, whatever. In fact, those cited were atheists and disowned Judaism and Jewish ethnicity as inimical to internationalism and community unity. It is also overlooked that most of these leaders of Jewish ancestry were liquidated in the purges of the thirties. Further, the large degree of "Jewish" involvement in the revolution is quite understandable because Czarist Russia had the largest Jewish population in Europe and strongly persecuted Jews. Financial aid from other Jews to relieve the plight of their persecuted brethren is not a mystery either. And the Jewish propensity to identify with the underdog and support liberal social causes is consistent with the fact that Jews had been a persecuted minority through the centuries.

But I was ignorant of these facts. I knew only the distorted "facts" of the radical Right. Thus, I came to view the Jew as the number-one enemy of mankind, an insidious pest that should be destroyed. As I absorbed more and more of this psychotic thinking, I developed a deepening hatred that slowly consumed me. I hated blacks, of course, as do all radical rightists, but I literally loathed Jews, who supposedly were the real masterminds and used the blacks as pawns.

Perhaps more significant than the content of my thinking at this stage was the new *mode* of thinking that I had developed. This ideological thinking is succinctly described by Burnham:

> A convinced believer in the anti-semitic ideology tells me that the Bolshevik revolution is a Jewish plot. I point out to him that the revolution was led to its first major victory by a non-Jew, Lenin. He then explains that Lenin was the pawn of Trotsky, Radek, Kamenev, and Zinoviev and other Jews who were in the Bolshevik High Command. I remind him that Lenin's successor as leader of the revolution, the non-Jew Stalin, killed off all those Jews; and that Stalin has been followed by the non-Jew, Khrushchev, under whose rule there have been notable revivals of anti-semitic attitudes and conduct. He then informs me that the seeming Soviet anti-semitism is only a fraud invented by the Jewish press, and that Stalin and Khrushchev are really Jews whose names have been changed with a total substitution of forged records. Suppose I am able to present documents that even he will have to admit show this to be impossible. He is still unmoved. He tells me that the real Jewish center that controls the revolution and the entire world conspiracy is not in Russia anyway, but in Antwerp, Tel Aviv, Lhasa, New York, or some-

where, and that it has deliberately eliminated the Jews from the public officialdom of the Bolshevik countries in order to conceal its hand and deceive the world about what is going on.

The militant segregationist also uses this style of thinking:

> I mention after hearing him assert the innate inferiority of the Negro race, the fact that in baseball, boxing, track and field sports, Negroes are the champions. These purely physical achievements, he explains, are proof of how close Negroes remain to animals in the evolutionary scale. I add the names of Negro musicians, singers, actors and writers of the first rank. Naturally, he comments, they carry over a sense of rhythm from the tribal dance and tom-tom ceremonies. I ask how many law graduates of his state university could stand up against Judge Thurgood Marshall; how many sociologists against Professor C. Eric Lincoln; how many psychologists against Professor Kenneth Clark? Doubtless all such have plenty of white blood, he answers, but in any case they are only exceptions to prove the general rule of inferiority; that is confirmed by the low intellectual attainments of the average Negro. I observe that the average Negro has been educated in worse schools, and for fewer years, than the average white. Of course, he agrees: No use wasting good education on low-grade material.

An ideologue—one who thinks ideologically— can't lose. He can't lose because his answer, his interpretation and his attitudes have been determined in advance of the particular experience or observation. They are derived from the ideology and are not subject to the facts. There is no possible argument, observation or experiment that could disprove a firm ideological belief for the very simple reason that an ideologue will not accept any argument, observation, or experiment as constituting disproof. (James Burnham, *Suicide of the West*, Arlington House, New Rochelle, New York, 1964, pp. 100–1.)

Once I made this transition from normal, rational thinking to ideological thinking, I became totally impervious to anything or anyone outside the ideology. I was now immunized against the outside world and lived in the impenetrable world of rightist ideology.

From September 1963 through early 1964 I studied these themes intensely and met regularly with radicals. Through these meetings I gradually made a number of radical friends who were the nucleus of a rightist underground in the area. One of those with whom I formed a fast friendship was a local NSRP officer and a member of the Minutemen as well. He was a pleasant guy who was devoted to the cause.

One night the leader of the Mobile chapter of the NSRP introduced me to two professional radicals at the organization's headquarters. They were friends of his and had recently moved to Mobile from Miami. Both were divorced and in their late thirties. One had been a pilot, and the other had been in business. They were part of a radical group in Miami that, because of pressures from law enforcement, left Miami to form an underground network throughout the South.

They were cautious about forming friendships. So our relationship developed more slowly than with others. They met with me on numerous occasions to discuss ideology and see how committed I was, but after several months we had become good friends.

An older couple in their sixties from the Miami area also were among the important rightists in the Mobile area. I spent many hours in their home discussing the "communist-Jewish conspiracy" and listening to tapes on its various aspects.

From these leaders, I learned many practical aspects of conducting clandestine activities. Everything was done in strict security. We would meet at prearranged rendezvous points, observing painstaking procedures to assure that we weren't being followed. Because of possible bugging, important matters were discussed only in secure places, hardly ever in our homes, offices, or automobiles. To circumvent FBI phone taps, we never discussed anything on the phone. Any references to meeting places or people were made in veiled terms or code words. These precautions greatly hampered our activities, but they were essential if we were to function at all.

The many hours we spent together discussing ideology, strategy, and tactics served to deepen our relationships and gave me a thorough foundation in rightist political theory and practice. As a result I felt even more strongly the need to give myself to this vital cause. Of course, this brought increasing acceptance, approval, and recognition, and drew me even more deeply into the cause.

The more conversant I became with right-wing ideas and doctrines, and the more radical and outspoken I was on the need for action, the more I was approved and recognized. The more skillful and professional I was in planning and implementing these ideas for action, the faster I rose in the estimation of right-wing leaders.

By early 1964 I had become well versed in rightist ideology and was a trusted member of the local group. In February, disenchanted with high school and eager for more direct action, I dropped out and went to Montgomery to meet with Admiral John Crommelin, a prominent right-wing leader who was a good friend of my colleagues.

Admiral Crommelin was a graduate of Annapolis and had been executive officer of the *Enterprise* during World War II. A gruff old man in his sixties, the admiral lived in retirement in Montgomery where he had a comfortable house as well as a large country estate, Harrogate Springs, about twenty-five miles out of town.

When I arrived in Montgomery on a cold, gray winter day, the admiral's wife was waiting for me at the station and she drove out to Harrogate Springs.

The admiral was in conference with several other rightists, but he cordially received me, showed me to a guest room, and returned to his visitors. Later that evening, and for several days, we talked about the "communist-Jewish conspiracy." Then I traveled on to NRSP national headquarters in Birmingham for a meeting with Dr. Edward Fields, the executive director. After a brief visit, I returned to Mobile and gave myself more passionately to the work of the cause.

During this time I gained a wider perspective of the radical Right—and also of the jealousy, bickering, and competition among rightist groups and leaders. For the first time it really hit me that the right wing was a fragmented movement that had little real unity.

CHAPTER SIX

My involvement in violence and terrorism began with relatively minor acts of political harassment. At first this took the form of theatening phone calls to the two rabbis in Mobile and to the local head of the Jewish Anti-Defamation League. Then I included black civil rights leaders in the area as well. However, this satisfied me for only a short time. Soon I was thinking in terms of action rather than words.

In high school this initially took the form of picking on some of the Jewish students. At first I used verbal abuse, calling them such things as "kikes" and "Jewish dogs" in the presence of their friends. Then I began to threaten them with violence. Finally I began hitting certain ones when I could. One Jewish boy, who was about my age, took the brunt of my anger. He was a mild-mannered guy and would never fight back no matter how much I hit him or what I said.

Had I known then how to build a bomb, I probably would have put one at the Jewish synagogue nearest my home, but I settled for harassment. Late one night I walked to the synagogue, which was only a few blocks from my grandmother's house where I was spending the weekend. After making certain that no one was around, I pulled out a can of red spray paint and painted swastikas on the building. Obviously this caused a furor among the Jews. In the weeks that followed I made scare calls to the synagogue during services.

Far from satisfying my hostility, this behavior only intensified it. So by the spring of 1964, after I had dropped out of school, some of my close friends and I were actively discussing even stronger acts of intimidation.

I also worked with a close friend, a member of the Minutemen, on compiling dossiers on major political enemies in the area. He had been quietly doing this for some time, and now the two of us pressed the effort to the point of even locating and reconnoitering the homes and offices of these people. Thus, the next step in the escalating pattern of violence was shooting into the houses of certain selected enemies. During my first eight to nine months in the radical Right I had purchased various firearms and diligently practiced marksmanship, which was strongly encouraged. So I was well prepared for this campaign.

We began by shooting into the houses of black civil rights leaders late at night. Usually one of us would drive, and the other would do the shooting. We struck when few people would be out to identify our car—but not so late that we would be conspicuous. On many occasions we struck while the police were changing shifts, sometimes using radios to monitor their frequencies. For months we waged a campaign of terror against the black community and even fired into the mayor's house on one occasion.

One of my most ambitious schemes during this time was to bomb the home of a state NAACP official in Mobile. This was planned for March 6, 1964, but was later canceled because of a security leak. According to FBI files, an "assistant special agent in charge of Army Intelligence, Mobile, was advised on March 2 as to this possible bombing."

Part of our strategy was to create fear in the black community—but it was more important to produce racial polarization and eventual retaliation. This retaliation would then swell the ranks of whites who would be willing to condone or employ violence as a viable response to the racial problem.

From our perspective this was a highly desirable and totally justified course of action—even though it might result in some casualties among whites. As long as harmonious race relations prevailed—and they did in Mobile—integration could proceed unhindered and eventually bring interracial marriage. Interracial marriage—the pollution of the master race (whites)—would spell the certain destruction of America and Western civilization; therefore, any preventive action was justified.

If the polarization and retaliation had occurred as we hoped, we planned to liquidate selected Jewish, white, and black leaders during the ensuing confusion. We also had a mobilization plan for responding to attack. If one of our friends or sympathizers was attacked by a black, or if a confrontation developed, he could call a central number that was printed on a card. From the central number, calls would go out to about a dozen persons, each of whom would alert another dozen, and so on. Heavily armed, each would respond to the alert by proceeding to the scene for appropriate action. This network plan was called the Christian Military Defense League.

As we met and conferred through the months, many response plans were discussed. One of the more interesting was designed for a riot situation. Three men would move into the riot area in a van or pickup truck in which a .30 or .50 caliber machine gun was mounted but hidden from view. One man would drive, one would operate the weapon, and the third would go out on foot a couple of blocks away to provoke a large crowd of blacks to chase him. He would then run back to the truck with the mob in fast pursuit. Once the mob was in range, the machine gunner would open fire, killing as many as possible before speeding away. Of course, this plan was never implemented, but it was seriously considered as an option if the occasion arose.

We discussed other terrorist tactics—some even more bizarre. They ranged from distributing the dismembered body of a key black leader around the black community to setting out booby traps in the black communities of Mobile. These would be nicely wrapped so that a pedestrian would think it was a lost gift. But when he picked it up it would explode. This was a tactic used by Algerian terrorists.

For various reasons none of these plans was ever used, but they show the thinking and attitudes of rightist radicals—not just in the South, but everywhere.

In August 1964, after about a year in the movement, I got into serious trouble for the first time. Late one night I was driving through the black section of Mobile with the local NSRP leader. The police saw us and were suspicious about white men being in a black community late at night. They pulled us over for a routine search and found a .38 caliber revolver and my sawed-off shotgun. Because the barrel was only fourteen and seven-eighths inches long—under the eighteen-inch minimum—I was in violation of the Federal Firearms Act.

Prior to this I had been questioned several times by Detective Captain Bill Lami of the Mobile Police Department about acts of violence in the area. Bill was a friend of my dad's and tried to warn me about what I was getting into. If only I had listened, . . . but I was stubborn and ignored him. Now what he predicted had come true. I was held for questioning and later charged by the U.S. government with federal firearms violation.

Through the efforts of our family attorney, Thomas Haas, and the mercy of U.S. District Judge Daniel Thomas, I was eventually placed on probation until my twenty-first birthday. In his sentencing remarks, the judge said that if he ever heard of my associating with another radical or touching another gun—even a shotgun for dove hunting—he would revoke my probation and send me to prison.

My arrest was in August 1964. Until the sentencing in May 1966, I was more active than ever—but also much more cautious. After the sentencing, however, I had no choice but to discontinue most of my activities and meet less frequently with my friends.

Early in the summer of 1967, I noticed that the FBI and police no longer were watching me closely. By now my thinking had matured some—at least to the extent of thinking more in strategic rather than tactical terms. Two things seemed clear to me. First, the radical Right could never hope to achieve its goals without high-level unity. This was practically nonexistent at the time. Second, rank-and-file right-wing radicals around the country needed to have a common identity. I was now almost twenty-one and an effective terrorist. I also knew some of the top leaders of the radical Right and had access to the others. By developing my relationships with the leaders and at the same time conducting a major anti-Jewish terrorist operation, I thought I could promote rightist unity. In any case I would be advancing my position and power in the movement.

With this in mind, in midsummer of 1967 I contacted Robert Shelton, Imperial Wizard of the United Klans of America*—largest of the Klan organizations—with head-

* FBI files report:

Records of Superior Court of Fulton County, Georgia, reflect that this Klan organization was granted a corporate charter on February 21, 1961, at Atlanta, Georgia, under the name United Klans, Knights of the Ku Klux Klan of America, Inc.

A source advised on February 27, 1961, that United Klans was formed as a result of a split in the U.S. Klans, Knights of the Ku Klux Klan, Inc. According to the source, the split resulted from a leadership dispute and United Klans has the same aims and objec-

quarters in Alabama. Because I had the recommendation
of a long-time Klan leader in South Alabama, it was a
relatively simple matter to arrange a meeting.

I drove to Tuscaloosa, Alabama, to meet with him.
After having coffee together at a downtown restaurant,
we drove to his comfortable lakeside home in Sherwood
Forrest. Here he lived with his family and conducted
Klan business. We talked for perhaps an hour, exchanging
thoughts on a variety of right-wing topics. I then returned
to Mobile, promising to keep in touch. I felt good about
the rapport that had been established and confident that
our relationship would mature in the days to come.

In a major speech before his constituents in the late sixties, Shelton articulated some of his convictions:

> We have given the Negroes an education, and
> what outcome have we reaped? Thousands and
> hundreds of thousands of Negro MORONS,

tives as the parent group. These are the promotion of Americanism,
white supremacy, and segregation of the races.

The first source and a second source advised in July, 1961, that
United Klans, Knights of the Ku Klux Klan of America, Inc.,
merged with Alabama Knights, Knights of the Ku Klux Klan. The
merged organization established headquarters in Suite 401, Alston
Building, Tuscaloosa, Alabama. (The organization is directed by
ROBERT SHELTON, Imperial Wizard, and is the dominant Klan
group in the South, with Units in several Southern states.)

Second source advised that at a meeting in Prattville, Alabama,
on October 22, 1961, the U.S. Klans, Knights of the Ku Klux Klan,
merged with the United Klans of America, Inc., Knights of the Ku
Klux Klan.

Third source advised on May 25, 1966, that the UKA is cur-
rently an active organization, with Klaverns in several states. This
source said that ROBERT M. SHELTON is the Imperial Wizard of
this organization and was elected to this position on September 5,
1964, at a National Klonvocation in Birmingham, Alabama. Source
stated that during April, 1966, the National Office was moved from
Suite 401, Alston Building, Tuscaloosa, Alabama, to the carport of
SHELTON's residence, #18 Lake Sherwood, Star Route, North-
port, Alabama, which space he had converted into a room.

THICK LIPPED, BULGY EYED, WINED UP, DOPED UP MORONS . . . laboring under the delusion that they have an education which makes them the equal of our white race. . . .

Yes, the Negro may wear a Palm Beach suit instead of the beads he stole from a neighboring village, he may carry a gold headed cane instead of a shrunken head, and he may use the telephone instead of his ancient drum, but is his MIND any less than that of a savage? And my friends, MIND is the man, for as a man thinketh, so he is, contrary to Karl Marx's theory that "A man is what he eats." The Negroes have been eating humans for years . . . but they are still animals!

I have no race prejudices my friends . . . for what the fools call race prejudice is the God implanted instinct of self preservation, the first law of nature.

There is not a hope, in faith or in reason, for the Negro outside of complete and total separation. . . .

On our side are the forces of freedom, liberty, racial integrity and white supremacy, led by the United Klans of America. On the other side are the forces of a communism, Black Nationalism, Socialism, which all come under the index of WORLD ZIONISM, the force that is using all these by-products to accomplish their objective. . . . (Excerpts from "Robert M. Shelton's Homecoming Address," *The Fiery Cross*, January 1970, pp. 7–11.)

Later that summer I drove to Laurel, Mississippi, to meet with Sam Bowers, Imperial Wizard of the White

Knights of the Ku Klux Klan in Mississippi.† Though initially suspicious, Sam accepted me and we became close associates after I had proven my trustworthiness. Because Sam was head of the most violent right-wing organization in America, he was the logical person with whom to work. Also, because Mississippi had so many local suspects to investigate, it would be a good place for an out-of-stater to operate without detection.

Sam was quite articulate and had a phenomenal memory and a mind for detail. Yet he was largely a closed person, and few knew him intimately. Strange as it may seem, Sam was a religious person as were most right-wing extremists.

Sam was often under surveillance by the FBI. So we had to meet under the most careful security procedures. We nearly always met at prearranged rendezvous points at night—usually in remote wooded areas. To assure that

† FBI files state:

A source advised that on February 15, 1964, approximately 200 members of the Original Knights of the Ku Klux Klan from the State of Mississippi met at Brookhaven, Mississippi. Those present decided to defect from the Original Knights and to form their own Klan group in Mississippi to be known as the White Knights of the Ku Klux Klan of Mississippi.

This source advised that the aims and purposes of the WKKKKOM are to preserve Christian civilization, protect and promote white supremacy and the segregation of the races, to fight Communism and to extend the dignity, heritage, and rights of the white race of America.

The same source advised on May 23, 1968, that the WKKKKOM is an unincorporated, secret organization existing in the State of Mississippi and formed for the sole purpose of preserving white supremacy regardless of the cost and including the use of force and violence. The official constitution and other directives of the organization do not openly advocate the use of force and violence; however, it is generally conceded among the members that in the end force and violence will be the salvation of the white man regarding his relationship with the Negro race.

we were not followed to our meeting places, we changed them frequently. Often we would leave our cars to talk so that our conversation would not be detected by transmitters hidden in our cars. On one occasion we met at Sam's office to discuss some important matters. Instead of talking we sat at a table and wrote out our thoughts on notebook paper and exchanged them. When we finished, Sam got a bucket of water, burned the papers, ground the ashes, placed them in the water, and flushed them down the toilet.

Clearly, our use of conversation was extremely well guarded. We were ever mindful of the FBI's highly sophisticated electronic monitoring equipment. On the telephone we were even more cautious, speaking only in veiled references and code words that both parties understood but no one else could decipher.

The great fear of FBI undercover agents, phone taps, and listening devices produced a near paralysis of paranoia in the Klan and other right-wing organizations. There were many ideas for violence and many people who would have participated in them, but everyone was reluctant to develop and implement them because they never could quite be sure who was an undercover agent. Had it not been for this fear of the FBI and its infiltration, there would have easily been ten times more violence in the sixties than actually occurred.

In September 1967, the Klan launched a terror campaign against the state's Jewish population as well as certain selected black and white leaders.

The first target was Temple Beth Israel in Jackson, Mississippi. On the evening of September 18, 1967, at about 10:30 P.M., a high-explosive device was detonated at the synagogue, doing major damage. Great fear spread throughout the Jewish community as the news made front-page copy around the nation and was a featured piece on network evening news.

FBI files indicate that about $25,000 worth of damage was done to the $460,000 building. A man who was driving past the synagogue at the time of the explosion heard a loud boom and saw debris flying in every direction from the northern end of the building.

A Jackson newspaper reported that the front double doors were destroyed, interior walls buckled, plaster strewn about, light fixtures downed, and most of the windows blown out on one side of the building.

The explosion rattled windows in houses one quarter of a mile away.

Next was Tougaloo College, a black institution near Jackson, Mississippi, which was considered a hotbed of subversion and communist activity by conservatives in Mississippi. In the early morning hours of October 6, 1967, a high-order explosive device was detonated at the campus house of Dr. William T. Bush, dean of the college.

An employee of the college said he was driving a panel truck in his patrol of the college when a heavy explosion shook the truck. He was about three hundred yards from the Bush house when it occurred, and he thought he would lose control of the vehicle, but fortunately he was able to stop and get out. Damage to the house was estimated at three thousand dollars.

Much publicity ensued, and fear began to grow in the black community as well.

A couple of weeks later another bomb exploded late in the evening at the house of Robert Kochtitzky, a local white minister and civil rights leader. Early in the morning of November 15, 1967, another bomb exploded at the home of the Reverend Allan Johnson in Laurel, Mississippi. The Reverend Johnson, a black, was former assistant state director of the NAACP and a leader of the Southern Christian Leadership Conference.

The FBI received testimony from one resident who was eating "an order of fish" when he heard the explosion. "What the heck is that?" he thought and ran to the door of the cafe. He saw "a lot of smoke and dust" in the direction of St. Paul's church where the Reverend Johnson ministered. Damages were estimated at between five and six thousand dollars.

Then, on the night of November 21, 1967, just after 11 P.M., a bomb was detonated at the home of Rabbi Perry Nussbaum of Beth Israel Synagogue, shattering the night air and doing seven thousand dollars' damage. By now terror was rampant in the Jewish and black communities and national news was focusing on Mississippi. J. Edgar Hoover sent additional FBI agents into Mississippi to assist with the investigations and the Anti-Defamation League increased its efforts.

December 20 was a cold, rainy day in Laurel, Mississippi. Sam and I met for one of our periodic strategy sessions. That night we drove to Collins, Mississippi, about twenty miles away. Our intention was to machine-gun the home of a local black who had fired on a police officer some days earlier. However, in the process of trying to locate his house we got our directions confused and pulled into a closed service station. The night marshal, Buster Lott, had been cruising around and saw us. So he pulled in to see what we were doing.

He noticed that I had Alabama tags so he asked to see my driver's license. When he discovered that I was from Alabama, he wanted to know why I was in that little town on a rainy, December night.

Then he wanted to talk to Sam. So he went up to the car and asked to see his driver's license. Evidently he recognized Sam's name. Whatever the reason, he decided to hold us for questioning.

Once we were in the county jail, he routinely searched our car and found a loaded .45 caliber submachine gun under a sweater on the front seat. The FBI and state police were called immediately and my cover was blown. Sam and I had been publicly linked. Soon the federal government would be seeking an indictment against me for possession of a submachine gun. Also, when the FBI checked out the serial number of my car, they found that it had been stolen several months before I bought it—one of the many cars "dumped" in Mississippi before title registration was required. So I was in possession of stolen property.

Nonetheless, Sam and I were released on bond the next day, and after the Christmas holidays, I began classes at Mobile College, hoping to present a better image to authorities. I kept a low profile as a student until early March.

In a few weeks a federal grand jury would release its indictments, and I had decided to go underground rather than fight a losing court battle. Sam would be able to testify that he didn't know the gun was in the car, and he would be found not guilty. It was my gun and my car. I clearly was guilty. So I began to prepare myself to be more useful when I went underground. I decided to take a trip to Los Angeles to deepen my ties with Dr. Wesley Swift, a leader in radical-Right circles. I also met with other right-wing leaders on the West Coast. In October I had talked with Dr. Swift and was invited to come to California and serve as his understudy for a time. I didn't have time for extended study now, so I decided on a short visit as the next best thing.

I spent a fruitful week and a half with Dr. Swift and his aide, Dennis Mowrer. As FBI files indicate, Dennis Patrick Mowrer in May 1967 assumed the duties as West Coast coordinator of the Minutemen organization and was then in the process of reorganizing the Minutemen and establishing a system of area coordination.

At that time Robert B. DePugh, chief of the Minutemen, was underground and being sought by the FBI. Swift, Mowrer, and I had detailed discussions on ideology, strategy, and tactics, and forged much deeper ties in the process.

Before returning home, I went to San Diego to visit my favorite uncle, a former vice-president of the Carnation Company. He now had his own business in San Diego, and I looked forward to visiting him and my cousins before going back to Mobile. Yet I found that I had nothing in common with them anymore. I had grown so distant from even my closest relatives that we could hardly communicate. The reason, of course, was my total obsession with the cause. It occupied all my thoughts and conversation and was the basis of all my relationships. Those who didn't share my ideology and commitment no longer were a real part of my life.

March 23 was a warm, sunny day in Mobile. I went down to Dauphin Island to swim and lie in the sun.

Upon returning home late that afternoon, I spotted FBI agents parked down the street watching my house. I didn't know exactly what they were up to, but I suspected that the indictment had come out. So instead of turning into our drive, I kept on going straight. Their car was facing toward mine, and the engine wasn't running. I just casually went straight as if I didn't see them, but they recognized me. Before they could turn their car around and catch up with me, however, I raced away, made several fast turns, and lost them.

This was it. The day I had long anticipated had now come. I immediately went to the house of a close friend and changed cars, then began making preparations for leaving the area at once. Meanwhile, a team of FBI agents was searching my parents' house and questioning my family concerning my possible whereabouts and plans.

A few days later I was in a safehouse in the mountains

of North Carolina, where I could safely relax and quietly wait for the heat to subside. The couple with whom I stayed was dedicated to the cause. They were part of the Miami group that had scattered throughout the South.

After several leisurely weeks had passed, I returned to Mississippi to meet with Sam. In strict secrecy, we discussed the political situation in the state and what our response should be. Before returning to North Carolina, I spent several more days meeting with key people.

During this period the Klan reign of terror continued with machine-gun and bombing attacks on black leaders.

In Meridian alone there had been eleven terrorist acts since January, including the burning of eight black churches. Then on May 28, 1968, the Jewish synagogue in Meridian, Mississippi, was bombed. Tension and fear were at an all-time high, and the FBI was intensely involved in investigating the situation, with J. Edgar Hoover phoning Mississippi each morning for progress reports.

May and June were particularly eventful months in this campaign and many federal agents were in the state. Thus, I spent a great deal of my time in North Carolina, but with great caution I returned to Mississippi in late June to coordinate planning and to direct the bombing of Meyer Davidson's house.

This then was the sequence of events leading up to our attempted bombing of Davidson's house that fateful June night.

CHAPTER SEVEN

After my sentencing I was returned to my cell, where I remained until December 13, 1968. About lunchtime on that day the jailor came to my cell and told me to get ready to leave for the Mississippi State Penitentiary at Parchman, Mississippi. I hurriedly packed the few things I had and was taken to the jailor's office where I was handcuffed to a chain that was wrapped around my waist. Five other men—three white and two black—were similarly chained. Then we were all taken downstairs to a prison station wagon used for transporting prisoners. It had a wire-mesh screen between the driver and passengers and covering the windows.

Because I was among those being transported, the State Highway Patrol took special measures to prevent my being rescued—or assassinated. Mississippi Highway Patrol cars in front of and behind us formed a convoy to escort us. Our speed was seldom less than eighty miles an hour, and as we passed certain checkpoints additional cars were waiting to relieve those that were accompanying us.

Cold, gray skies contributed to my gloominess as we left Meridian, which is in the east central part of the state. We proceeded north through the beautiful rolling hillside around Philadelphia. It was near here that the three civil rights workers, James Chaney, Andrew Goodman, and Michael Schwerner, were murdered by the Klan in 1963. From Philadelphia we went northward to Kosciusko and then west toward Greenwood—the hometown of Byron de la Beckwith who was tried but never convicted for the assassination of Medgar Evers, a black civil rights leader in Mississippi. As we got closer to Greenwood the road began to level off and we entered the flat land of the Mississippi delta, one of the richest farming areas in the United States. From Greenwood it was just a short piece to U. S. 49, the highway to Parchman.

I had never been to the delta before, and as I looked at the passing fields I felt deep despair. All I could see was miles of stark brown cotton stalks, which had been stripped by pickers, dotted by a few white bolls of cotton that had been missed. Ramshackle shanties were scattered here and there—often unpainted, with trash, weeds, and abandoned cars in the yard. In sharp contrast were the occasional stately southern homes, surrounded by well-manicured lawns and shade trees, with shiny Lincoln Continentals in the driveways. The thousands of acres of cotton fields belonged to wealthy delta planters who lived in these elegant houses, and the shanties were occupied by their fieldhands and the other laborers. Here, truly, are the last remnants of that enchanted world of the Old South.

As we moved farther into the delta with its miles of flat bleak land, my despair increased. I felt as if I were approaching the outermost edges of the earth—as if I would soon be cut off from civilization altogether.

Late that afternoon, just as it was becoming dark, we reached the Mississippi State Penitentiary at Parchman. I recall it vividly. It's not the kind of thing a person can easily forget. Unlike most prisons, which are compact and surrounded by a high wall, Parchman is a penal farm, a sixteen-thousand-acre farm much like a military reserva-

tion. The inmates were housed in twenty-two widely separated barracklike compounds, situated at various points
on the grounds. Each compound, called a camp, housed
an average of 100 to 175 men and was a self-contained
unit. The large brick buildings contained two large open
dormitories, a kitchen, dining hall, and bathing areas.
Outside was a four- or five-acre yard large enough for
football, baseball, and basketball. Surrounding all this was
an eight-foot heavy-duty storm fence topped with barbed
wire and guard towers on each corner.

We turned directly onto the prison grounds, which bor-
dered Highway 49 for about two miles. After passing a
brick guard station at the entrance, we proceeded down
a two-lane blacktop road called "guard row." On either
side were frame houses, one right after another a hundred
feet apart. Here lived the guards and other employees in
a sequestered community largely untouched by time and
modern society. In the windows and over the doors were
Christmas decorations and lights—red, green, yellow,
white, and blue. No doubt the families in those homes
were busily preparing for Christmas with increasing excitement. In just a few days these people would be caught
up in holiday festivities, but for me, this season of joy
would bring only depression because I couldn't be part of
it now or for years to come. Inside I felt a deep pang of
anguish recollecting the many happy and bounteous
Christmases I had spent at home with my family in Mobile. I shall never forget my feeling that evening as I rode
through guard row immersed in these thoughts.

We had driven a little more than a mile down guard
row when we reached the hospital, a large old one-story
red brick building surrounded by a tall fence and guard
towers. The gate was swung open long enough for us to
drive through, then locked again. We were now securely
in Parchman prison—long known as one of the worst prisons in the United States.

Now would begin the dehumanizing though necessary ritual of processing. We were all taken into the reception room where our chains and handcuffs were removed. The door was shut and locked behind us by Sgt. P. O. Miller, the man in charge of the hospital and receiving office. Sergeant Miller was an abrupt person who said little, but when he spoke there was no doubt who was in charge.

We were all ordered to line up side by side, strip naked, and put our clothes in a pile in front of us. Then we were made to assume various postures in order to permit a visual inspection. We even had to show the bottoms of our feet. Once the sergeant was satisfied that no one was concealing contraband on his person, we were each issued underwear, towels, three pairs of jeans, and three khaki shirts. Then we were told to dress out. Everyone except me (for some unknown reason) had all his hair cut off.

By now it was time for supper, and we were directed to the dining hall in the back of the hospital. Surprisingly enough, the food was fairly good. There was a lot of fresh milk, meat, bread, and vegetables.

After supper we were given blood tests and a routine physical examination, then placed in a receiving ward— actually the sick ward of the hospital, which also doubled as a receiving ward.

Later that night, after my processing had been completed, I was taken to the maximum security unit. I had assumed that I would remain at the hospital with the other prisoners pending assignment to a camp. That was the normal procedure. However, because of my notoriety prison officials were taking no chances with me. They did not want me to escape, and the maximum security unit was known as "little Alcatraz" because it was so secure, the safest place to house me. It was also feared by inmates because of the brutality that occurred there.

Separated from even my riding companions, I felt the

extreme hopelessness of my situation as I was driven to the maximum security unit. It was a well-lit concrete, brick, and steel building located in a flat, barren area surrounded by a twelve-foot fence topped with barbed wire and tall brick guard towers on each corner. The maximum security unit seemed to represent isolation—even from the prison farm itself. When we reached the entrance to the compound, the guards placed their guns in a depository; then the huge electric gate slowly rolled open, closing again as soon as our car passed through.

The building itself looked sinister and forbidding. It was a long, one-story, red brick structure with a low, flat roof. Just below the roof line a row of barred eighteen-inch windows ran the length of the building. In the middle was an electronically operated access door of heavy steel gratework. This opened into a central control area that separated the building into two wings, east and west. In the front part of the control area was an office and a receiving area. Telephones, intercoms to the guard towers, a powerful shortwave radio, and the electronic control panel for various doors were located there.

Farther back were three sets of sliding electric doors that formed compartments when closed. The second was about fifteen feet beyond the first, forming a holding area. The third, about thirty feet past the second, opened into the kitchen area. On either side of the second compartments were solid steel doors into the cellblocks.

I was brought into the receiving area and again made to strip naked. But this time I was also made to spread my legs apart and bend over for further inspection. This was extremely humiliating to say the least. All my newly issued prison clothes were taken, and I was given a set of long underwear and a blanket. I was then escorted by staff and trusties to my cell on death row. I had an eerie feeling as I walked down the cellblock corridor with men looking out at me from each cell as I passed. We stopped about three cells from the end. Slowly the door rolled open and I went in. Then it shut with a solid, definite clang.

The cellblock consisted of a ten-foot-wide corridor about a hundred feet long with a double shower stall and thirteen cells opening into it. Each cell was a concrete cubicle approximately six by nine feet with gray steel bars across the front and a sliding door that was operated from a control panel at the entrance to the cellblock. A six-inch concrete wall separated each cell. At the top of the corridor wall across from the cells was a narrow row of windows that went the length of the cellblock. The upper half of the walls was painted white and the lower half light green. The floor was plain, smooth concrete. Seven or eight incandescent 150-watt light bulbs were spaced along the corridor ceiling.

Although this was death row, only five of the men here actually had death sentences pending. The others were ordinary prisoners who had to be locked up for their own safety or because they were escape risks. They simply were kept on death row as a matter of convenience for the staff.

The other three cellblocks in the maximum security unit were used for punishment. Prior to my arrival at Parchman, officials were reported to have sent prisoners they regarded as disciplinary problems to the maximum security unit. Here they would be locked in a cell without a mattress or cover—only a bare steel bunk, commode, and face bowl. In those days the starvation diet, for hard cases, consisted of two meals a day: a cup of coffee and two biscuits with sorghum molasses for breakfast and a one-inch square of corn bread and one teaspoon of black-eyed peas for supper. Individuals who were especially troublesome were placed in the dark hole, a cell that was six feet square, completely enclosed, and pitch dark when the door was closed. They received only water and a slight food ration. Toilet facilities were built into the floor and consisted of an eight-inch hole level with the floor, which could be flushed by a button on the wall.

Although officials had largely phased out harsh discipline of unruly prisoners by the time of my incarceration, there were still reports of what might be considered excessive punishment. During the winter officials might use an ordinary garden hose to spray everyone down until they were soaking wet, then open the windows and turn on the powerful overhead exhaust fan. The effect of the strong draft of cold air on wet bodies was highly effective. A few hours of this treatment would quiet down even the hardest and toughest of men. During the summer the technique was reversed. The exhaust fans, which normally ran day and night during the summer, were turned off. The hot-box effect then served equally well to subdue the unruly.

In some cases officials and trusties would even enter the cells of certain "hard cases" and beat the men down with blackjacks. They would give a strong laxative to others and handcuff them to the bars of their cells with their hands cuffed so high up on the cross bars that they had to stand on tiptoe. When the laxative began to take effect it was an extremely miserable situation. Every time a man was sent to the maximum security unit for punishment, his head was shaved before he was taken to his cell.

These things were common until about the time I came, 1968. In fact, as late as 1964 men were regularly whipped with "the bull hide"—also called "Black Annie." This was a thick leather strap one quarter of an inch thick and about six inches wide and four feet long. Usually ten hard licks would be administered to the naked buttocks of a man while four trusties held him down—one on each arm and leg. The "hide" was dreaded by everyone and could tame even the strongest of men.

Fortunately, these abuses were on the way out when I

came to Parchman. The official policy of the new superintendent, Tom Cook, was to discontinue corporal punishment. Some of the hard-line, old-guard officials still tried to use these methods on occasion but eventually realized that they couldn't get away with it anymore.

Not long after I had settled down in my cell, the man to my left told me that his name was Johnny Nettles and that he was being held for "safekeeping." Nettles had also been in prison in Louisiana. He asked my name and where I was from. He then passed the word to the others in the cellblock. Everyone knew about me, of course, because they had been reading the newspaper and listening to the radio. I was a celebrity of sorts—the top Klan terrorist who had shot a policeman (with a submachine gun, no less) in a wild gun battle. It must have been something of a surprise to them to discover that I was quiet, reserved, and aloof.

Of the five men with death sentences, three were black and the other two white. The remaining six who were there for safekeeping were evenly divided racially.

One of the white men under death sentence for first-degree murder was Phillip Yates. Phillip, twenty-six, was a handsome young man, about six feet tall. Although intelligent and well read, he was outspoken and had a violent temper, which was easily provoked. He was from Lucedale, in rural Mississippi, about thirty miles from Mobile, where his parents had been dairy farmers. He had been convicted of murdering a man just a few miles from his home and had been on death row for five years while appealing his case. Eventually he, along with the other four, would beat the death penalty and be resentenced to life in prison.

Gerald Irving was another of those under the death sentence. He was a short, fat black man in his early twenties. Gerald was sometimes loud, blustery, and obnoxious, but he usually was friendly and willing to help anyone who asked. He had been convicted of killing and raping the eighty-year-old mother of a federal judge in Gulfport, Mississippi.

One of the nicest people I met at Parchman was Claude Shinall. He was a quiet, mild-mannered, easygoing guy in his late twenties. He, too, was black. Claude was convicted of killing a constable near Hattiesburg, Mississippi. From all indications the constable, a white man, provoked Claude into what he did. Prison authorities had a high regard for him—so high, in fact, that a couple of years later his sentence was commuted and he was assigned to work at the governor's mansion.

The other white man on death row, Burl Rouse of Pascagoula, Mississippi, was a bald, stocky man in his forties. He had killed his wife and stepdaughter in a drunken rage, which he said he couldn't even remember. Burl had earlier murdered his first wife and was sentenced to life in prison in Louisiana. However, he had been paroled after ten years.

Then there was the Witch Doctor—John Henry Morgan. He was a black man in his late forties. Stocky, strong, quiet, and rumored to practice witchcraft, he had been convicted of assaulting a white couple whose car was parked on the levy of the Mississippi River near Greenville. He had murdered the man and kidnapped his wife. Somehow she lived to testify against him, and he was sentenced to life plus fifteen years.

The other men who were housed on death row were inmates who had escaped or were in protective custody. One fellow, for example, was a psychiatric case and was awaiting transfer to the state mental hospital. Another had escaped and been recaptured. Another had informed on someone and had to be locked up for his own protection.

Albert Lepard was convicted of burning his aunt's house while she was in it. He had a life sentence and thirty-five years. He had escaped numerous times but always was recaptured. A scrawny, short, red-headed Irishman with a violent temper, he came from a poor white rural Mississippi background.

I was confined to my cell twenty-four hours a day—as was everyone else on death row. Twice a week we were allowed out for thirty minutes to shower and shave. It was a very restrictive existence to say the least.

The cell itself was a drab, dismal place—reminiscent of a stall in a dog kennel. The concrete walls were faded green on the lower half, dull white on the upper half, and covered with graffiti—names of those who had been in the cell and the dates, curse words, maxims, and so forth. The commode and face bowl, once white porcelain, were now dull, stained, and dirty. A dirty mattress was on the steelframe bunk and a large, heavy quilt provided warm covering. Otherwise the cell was as bare as the smooth concrete floor.

It did not take me long to realize that the worst thing about prison life was the boredom—nowhere to go and nothing to do. It is a very difficult adjustment for a normal, active person. My activities were limited to talking, reading, and thinking—all of which grow old quickly. One can't help but do a lot of thinking, and this often produces frustration and despair or self-pity.

To escape temporarily from the unpleasant reality of the cell, prisoners resorted to small portable radios and reading material—usually Westerns, detective stories, or sex books.

Breakfast, served about 6 A.M., consisted of either hot cakes, bacon, oatmeal and molasses or eggs, grits, sausage, biscuits, and peach preserves, with all the milk and coffee one could drink. The afternoon meal, served around 3 P.M., usually consisted of pork or beef in some form, corn bread and vegetables such as turnips, Irish potatoes, yams, beans, squash, and a dessert and milk. Various fresh fruits and vegetables were also served in season.

My initial stay on death row was quite brief, lasting less than two weeks. No doubt it would have been much longer had it not been for a peculiar incident that occurred about ten days after my arrival.

It was December 23. Only three days earlier I had celebrated my twenty-second birthday on death row. So I was not in high spirits when to my surprise the warden, Tom Cook, and two chaplains, W. D. Kirk and Selby McManus, came in to give everyone a Christmas gift and hold a brief service. They had been in the cellblock only a few minutes when I began to hear Phillip Yates shouting heatedly. A few moments later I heard sounds of porcelain shattering against the bars and out in the corridor. In an angry rage, Yates had somehow kicked his commode loose from the wall and was throwing the broken pieces at the warden and chaplains. Others immediately followed his lead as the warden and chaplains fled to safety in the doorway of the cellblock. A few minutes later smoke began filtering down the corridor from mattresses that had been set afire. The guards moved quickly to activate the powerful ventilator system and flooded the cellblock with water, thus bringing the riot under control.

About an hour later, after the fury had subsided, Sgt. Alton Peaks, who was in charge of the maximum security unit, walked down the corridor to assess the damage. All but three commodes in the cellblock had been destroyed —broken up and used as missiles to pommel the warden.

When the sergeant came by, he noted that my cell was intact and orderly. I had not participated in the riot. Even if I had known the grievance and the intended protest (which I did not), I would not have taken part. From a purely pragmatic standpoint, such an effort was absolutely futile and hadn't the slightest chance of producing any gains. Moreover, I had never been one to follow the herd. As paradoxical as it may seem, I had always respected authority—although I had often disobeyed it when it conflicted with my ideological beliefs.

This was one aspect of my thinking that few people really understood or knew about. Although my radical activities at times brought me into open conflict with the law of the land and those enforcing it, I was basically pro-law and pro-law enforcement. My disagreement was not with the system as a whole nor with those involved in it. In fact, I had always been in awe of both. My problem was with what I considered a few bad laws that were ruining our country—the civil rights laws.

In any event, I did not join the riot. As a result, the warden transferred me and two other men to the hospital unit where I was given a job as laboratory technician trainee.

CHAPTER EIGHT

My transfer to the hospital was an unexpected boon. Although the security was tighter than any other unit of the prison except the maximum security unit, the general living conditions were much better than elsewhere.

I lived in a small dormitory room with about a dozen other guys who also worked at the hospital. Our room had its own TV and bathroom and was fairly comfortable—although short on space. It was much cleaner than any of the other camps, and the food was much better.

The sergeant in charge of the hospital, Paul Miller, presented a rather gruff, intimidating image. But he was a nice guy beneath the surface. This made things better still.

The work of a laboratory technician was completely foreign to me, and I didn't particularly like it. But it was a good job in terms of the fringe benefits (living at the hospital), and I learned rapidly. My teacher was another inmate who had held the job for several years and was soon to be paroled. Although this journeyman-apprentice approach was rather crude in such a complicated field, I was able to learn the basics fairly well in a short time.

My work day began with breakfast at 5:00 A.M. and consisted of routine laboratory operations—urinalyses, white-cell counts, hemoglobin, hematocrit, glucose tolerance, and other testing procedures. These were performed on those who were hospital patients and those coming in for "sick call." In addition each new inmate entering the prison was given a blood test for VD and had his blood typed.

Naturally, I was in daily contact with the prison physician, Dr. Luther McCaskill, who also was an inmate. He had been convicted of performing an illegal abortion on a woman who later died from complications. A black man, Dr. McCaskill was about thirty-five years old, fat, jovial, and very likeable. He had a good personality and was a genuinely compassionate man who was respected by the inmates and staff. Although he knew my background of racism and violence, it didn't seem to matter to him. He befriended me and gave me the best medical treatment he could when I needed it.

I think our friendship had a deep influence on my racial views. As Dr. Mac and I came to know each other better, my attitudes about blacks began to mellow somewhat—not a lot, but it was a start at least. Such relationships usually are crucial in breaking prejudice and stereotyped thinking. At any rate, Mac and I became good friends.

Living and working in the prison hospital gave me firsthand knowledge of the darker side of prison life. Shootings, stabbings, and beatings were not infrequent, nor was homosexual rape. Critically wounded prisoners were often brought to the hospital from the camps or the fields.

In those days Parchman operated under the trusty system. Trusties were simply inmates who were selected by prison officials to serve as armed guards. They carried guns and functioned just like a civilian guard. In return for their services, trusties were given many privileges. They had considerable freedom. In fact, trusties were free to go and come on prison grounds without an escort, could drive prison vehicles, and could fish or hunt on the grounds during off-duty hours. They also had special living quarters separate from the other inmates and were never locked up. Each year at Christmas they were allowed to go home on a ten-day holiday leave. They also were generally fed better than the average prisoner and were permitted to have items that others were denied for security reasons. In short, being a trusty made prison life much more bearable than would otherwise be the case.

Trusties were selected by the camp sergeant and had to be approved by the superintendent or assistant superintendent. The sergeant could also strip a trusty of his rank at will and little recourse was available. This arrangement served to make trusties dependent on the sergeant's goodwill and produced an almost unquestioning obedience to his orders—right or wrong. This was doubly reinforced because when a trusty was stripped of his status he was placed back into the regular prison population —with the very men he guarded (and many times mistreated).

Since its beginning in the 1890s Parchman had been a prison farm, and those confined there were compelled to do farm work. This chiefly consisted of planting, hoeing, and harvesting cotton and various vegetable crops—by hand. Only in the mid-sixties did tractors and mechanical cotton pickers begin to replace manual labor, and then only slowly. Often one could see a phalanx of 100 to 150 men moving through the field side by side picking or hoeing cotton. Arduous labor continued relentlessly year around—from daylight to dark, five and a half days a week, in a hundred plus degree temperatures in summer to twenty degree temperatures in winter.

The inmates, quite naturally, hated the system. Sometimes they would refuse to work and other times they would work slowly. Some, of course, just couldn't keep up with the grueling pace and rigorous conditions. To speed up those who worked slowly—and to coerce those who stopped—the trusties would fire thirty-thirty rifle rounds in the vicinity of the prisoners. Sometimes men would be hit by the rifle fire, usually because of poor aim or ricochet—but sometimes deliberately. Not until the late sixties did these conditions begin to change.

The wounded were brought to the hospital for treatment and were returned to the field if at all possible.

Most of the serious injuries, however, were the result of conflicts among the inmates themselves, and this is primarily what I saw and helped treat. Stabbings, cuttings, and beatings were common. These incidents frequently originated over homosexual relationships or drunken arguments.

Homosexual love affairs were at the root of much of the violence among inmates. The homosexuals at the prison usually were quite promiscuous, and this tended to create jealousy when one partner had more than a passing interest in the other—which was often the case. As a result homosexuals were forever embroiled in highly complex relationships that could easily lead to squabbling and violence. I remember one instance in which a man was stabbed in the chest and abdomen because of a homosexual love quarrel. Someone apparently had tried to steal the affections of his lover, and in the ensuing fight he was almost killed. In a similar situation an inmate was attacked in his sleep and beaten on the head with a heavy iron bar. He miraculously survived but was permanently blinded.

Drinking also caused conflict among the inmates. There were prisoners in every camp devoted to the manufacture, consumption, and sale of home brew. This was usually made by fermenting potatoes or apples or raisins in a solution of sugar and water. After three or four days a potent beverage resulted. To speed the process and improve the product, yeast was used when it was available. It was a constant matching of wits for the inmates to find the containers, raw materials, and places to make their home brew, but somehow they generally succeeded. Often it was made by kitchen personnel, or at least with their help, because they had access to the needed supplies. Brew was found everywhere from footlockers to attics to holes carefully dug and camouflaged in the yard. Containers ranged from cooking pots to wash pails and mop buckets. On one occasion, someone even used a high-topped rubber boot.

Prison officials were always on the lookout and searching for brew because it caused so much trouble. In the tense, charged atmosphere of a prison, drinking is very dangerous. It lowers inhibition and tolerance levels to the point where hostile impulses are more easily expressed.

In addition to enjoying the benefits of their labors, these inmates also took great pride in outwitting the system. Unfortunately, such conniving frequently caused trouble.

For example, I was working in the lab one day when two men were rushed to the emergency room from one of the camps. As they were wheeled down the corridor blood was spurting everywhere. One was the camp cook and the other was the baker. They had been drinking and got into a fight with long, sharp butcher knives. The cook's arm was laid open like a ham that had been boned. His nerves and tendons had been severed and his arm was just hanging. The baker had been stabbed in the chest and abdomen and was gushing blood, barely alive. Fortunately both survived, although each required several operations before he was well.

Several years later at another camp, I had to intervene personally when one drunk inmate pulled a knife on another after a relatively minor disagreement. The one with a knife was chasing the other through the camp. Fortunately, he slowed down long enough for me to talk with him, and he came to his senses and gave me the knife. Minutes later, security officers arrived and took them both to maximum security.

Because any inmate (except those in maximum security) could come to the hospital for sick call, it was the central point for drug transactions. These drugs were obtained by theft from the pharmacy and by purchases or gifts from patients for whom they were prescribed or from visitors of inmates.

My assignment to the hospital was a real blessing in a way that I didn't realize at the time. Because the hospital was my initial assignment, I was able to avoid the pressures of adjustment. Here I found a more intelligent, higher caliber of inmate and much less group pressure than there were in the other camps where conformity to the group was necessary for acceptance and security.

Generally new inmates adopt the attitudes (feigned or unfeigned) of the prison subculture (toward society, staff, and other inmates). Eventually these new inmates also absorb the values of the subculture as well. This is often necessary for survival in such a hostile environment, but unfortunately it has dire consequences for survival outside of prison. Many of those who become acculturated to prison life are not aware that they have these attitudes and values when they return to the free world. Inevitably such attitudes and values produce conflict and difficulty in dealings with others. Thus, released inmates often have a hard time readjusting and unlearning these ways. Many simply do not succeed. They get themselves into situations that assure their return to prison—where the pattern is made stronger still.

Fortunately I did not fall into this subtle trap—partly because of my being at the hospital, but also because of my self-righteous and "holier than thou" attitude toward the inmates. I looked on them for the most part as a bunch of thugs, hoodlums, and reprobates from the lower class. This was, admittedly, a terrible attitude to have toward these people, and later it changed, but the truth is that I did feel this way at the time. As a result I kept myself aloof from most of them and didn't identify with the inmate subculture. The few I did associate with were generally intelligent, middle-class, noncriminal types—men who were basically decent but who had made a mistake.

One of those whom I liked and respected was Doug Ladner. Before being convicted and sentenced on charges of killing his wife, Doug was a family man who worked at a Veterans Administration Hospital. While in prison he was assigned to the hospital's emergency room. The doctors and officials recognized Doug as being almost as competent as a physician in diagnosing and treating medical problems. Many of the officials and their families came to him for treatment when the doctor was not in. An easygoing man of sound and mature judgment, Doug's main hobby was training bird dogs and this he continued to do (for prison officials). He was the kind of man who could be trusted as a friend.

During the six months that I spent at the hospital unit, my parents drove from Mobile nearly every visiting day (the first and third Sundays of the month). It was an exhausting trip of about 350 miles each way—all to spend just three hours with me. Mom and Dad both worked, and it was quite a strain on them to get up at 4 A.M. Sunday morning, drive to Parchman, then turn around after three hours and drive back, getting home after midnight. Each time they came they would bring my favorite snack foods—apricot nectar, cashew nuts, fig newtons, and so forth—and magazines—*U.S. News and World Report, National Review, National Observer, Time, Newsweek,* and so forth. It was a great encouragement to see my parents so often. It really helped keep up my morale. Their visits reminded me that there was hope, and that the horrible prison environment did not have to dominate me.

In spite of appearances, I was not quietly adjusting to prison life. I had no intention whatever of remaining at Parchman. I was merely biding my time while analyzing the security system for weaknesses that might facilitate my escape.

Once I gained a thorough working knowledge of the general security operations of the prison and of the hospital in particular, I began planning an escape. By smuggling sealed letters out to my associates, I was able to begin organizing and coordinating the effort that would soon secure my freedom.

My being in the hospital, however, didn't mean that officials now felt I could be trusted not to escape or misbehave. The truth is that they weren't sure exactly what to expect, but they wanted to give me a chance to "prove myself." So they took a "wait and see" attitude. At first I was observed rather closely, but by late spring they had relaxed, assuming that I was settling down and adjusting to prison life.

Perhaps one thing that contributed to this as much as anything was my attitude toward prison officials. I had been raised to respect older persons and those in positions of authority. Although I was at times mischievous in school, I was always respectful of my teachers and those in charge. My defiance of authority began when authority placed itself on the side of federal intervention to integrate—the policy of an ideology I viewed as un-American. My problem with authority was not a problem with authority per se but with authority defending an unjust cause. I wanted to be on the side of proper authority and felt that such officials should be on my side. In any event, my attitude toward prison officials, who largely shared my racial and political views, was very positive. This was in contrast to the majority of inmates, who in varying degrees seemed to have a sullen, resentful attitude toward authority.

Therefore, prison officials grew more confident in their attitude toward me. Although I was friendly to the officials and liked some of them very much, I certainly had no intention of remaining in prison. As I saw it, America was being undermined by the communist-Jewish conspiracy, and I needed to be free and in the thick of the battle against it. Many people were content to study and speak out about it; but I felt that the time had come for action, and that those few of us who were action oriented were vitally needed to press the terror campaign until it caught on elsewhere.

After exploring all possibilities, I came to the conclusion that a successful escape would require the assistance of one or two other inmates within the hospital. The first person was not hard to find. His name was Louis Shadoan, a clerk in the ID office. He was highly intelligent—with an I.Q. of 160 plus (according to officials). Louis, forty-six, was of medium build, with graying brown hair, blue eyes, and ruddy complexion. He had worked as a journalist at various times in life but his real profession was robbing banks. He had robbed quite a few in the Midwest and West and took pride in this skill.

When Louis finished his sentence at Parchman he would have to return to federal prison for violating his parole on a bank robbery charge. So he was ready and willing to join me in an escape. We began our planning in Louis' office.

Together we carefully observed the day-to-day operation of the hospital unit, noting in detail times and manner of garbage pickup, supply deliveries, changing of the guard, and so forth. We decided that the route of least resistance would be to overpower the inside night watchman late one evening and bribe one or more of the outside tower guards. The hospital closed at 5 P.M., and until five the next morning there was only one free-world guard on duty in the compound. His job consisted of supervising the inmate guards, dispensing medicine at scheduled times, and calling medical personnel in to handle after-hours emergencies.

This particular guard, George Miller, was slow, quiet, short, slightly overweight, and in his fifties. Overcoming him would be a relatively simple matter.

Once the basic plan had been agreed on, we began to move into more intensive planning. The escape would have three distinct phases. First, we would have to leave the hospital compound safely; second, we would have to reach a secure hideout; and third, we would go our separate ways to final destinations.

Plans for implementing phase one went smoothly. Louis began cultivating a good rapport with the trusty on one of the two front guard towers with the intention of bribing him at the proper time. I contacted a reliable inmate I knew and secured a map of the terrain and roads around the sixteen-thousand-acre (seven miles by four miles) prison farm. With this we could plan for our pickup. Louis and I then began compiling a list of supplies we would need once we were free. Arms, ammunition, grenades, food, clothing, camping gear, and various other items such as radio monitoring equipment and medical supplies were included.

The second phase, getting from the prison grounds to our hideout, presented no problems at all. I established and maintained contact with a close Klan colleague by smuggling letters in and out. He and another close friend began securing the list of supplies right away from sporting stores and surplus centers. In addition, they began making trips to the Parchman area to reconnoiter the prison grounds in general and the hospital unit in particular.

On one of these reconnaissance missions he made his

way to within a stone's throw of the hospital compound. On another occasion one of them had car trouble on an early morning in July near Inverness, Mississippi, some forty miles from Parchman. County sheriff's deputies, the highway patrol, and the FBI investigated but apparently did not connect the incident with any escape planning.

As Louis and I continued to plan our escape we both recognized the need for a third person to assure adequate manpower in taking over the hospital. Any fewer personnel would increase the chance of resistance on the part of the guards and night watchman. After serious consideration, we decided that we could safely approach Malcolm Houston, twenty-nine, an inmate-orderly in one of the wards. He had brown hair, brown eyes, a fair complexion, and medium build. Malcolm had attempted to escape before, though unsuccessfully, and we felt that he would be interested. Louis, who knew him better than I, made the initial approach, and found Malcolm receptive. Then I talked with him. We both felt that he was the man we needed and included him in our plans.

By this time our free-world accomplices had secured all needed supplies, carefully reconnoitered the prison area, and secured a safe place for our hideout in rural Rankin County just outside Jackson, Mississippi.

All that we needed to do now was coordinate the time of our pickup. This was crucial. We had to know for sure that they would be at the rendezvous point before making our break. Because unforeseen developments could arise to keep them from being there, we had to confirm it on the day of the escape. Phone calls in or out of the prison were forbidden. We had to devise an alternative means of communication. Smuggled letters were too slow, and walkie-talkies were too risky. A newspaper was the only other source of daily communication accessible to us. So we decided that they would place a classified ad in the Jackson *Daily News,* an evening paper, on the day they would be at the rendezvous point. If placed early in the morning, the ad would appear in the afternoon edition. And the afternoon edition was delivered to the hospital each day. The ad would be completely innocent to everyone but Louis and me; it would read: "Lost: German shepherd. Name Sam. Black and Silver in Color. Large Size." It would also include my associate's phone number. This would be our signal that they would be at the spot that night.

Even if our accomplices were able to be at the rendezvous point, unforeseen developments might prevent us from attempting an escape. So we needed some flexibility in the schedule. We set three consecutive days for them to be waiting for us. If we didn't make our break the first night, then we could fall back on the second or third. They would be there each night.

CHAPTER NINE

Wednesday, July 23, was a hot, muggy day, the first of three possible days for an escape.

I followed business-as-usual procedures, but with the pleasant thought that this would be my last day in prison, I felt a special excitement. Soon I would be free and active again.

There was tension, of course, because of the dangers involved, yet I had unbounded confidence in my skill, planning, and competence. I didn't think about the alternatives. I anticipated problems and planned appropriately through analytical review. But I did not dwell on the problems or doubt the success of the project. I had the objective, and I pursued it relentlessly.

Several times that morning, however, I pushed my chair away from the desk and walked to Louis' office, the next door down the hall on the right. I also went the other way to Malcolm's office. These visits usually were short because the doctor sent patients to me for tests throughout the day. We could not afford an extended discussion.

Obviously all of us tried to be inconspicuous, but it seemed like the hours would never pass. As morning gave way to afternoon my tension and excitement increased. I waited expectantly for the newspaper to arrive.

It was now close to 5 P.M., and the paper would be delivered any moment. We waited, but it didn't come. Time seemed to stand still. We continued to wait. But still no paper. It was getting serious. We were ready to move as soon as it got dark, but we didn't know if our colleagues would be on the road with the getaway car. If we escaped and got to the rendezvous point and they were not there, we would surely be recaptured and probably killed. Our predicament was crucial. If the paper was not delivered soon we would have to switch to another night. So we waited anxiously.

Usually a trusty made the deliveries. He had a paper route and delivered newspapers for subscribers at all the camps, houses, and administrative buildings on the farm. Finally he came with the two or three copies that were delivered to the hospital. Louis asked to look at one and came by my office with it under his arm. I saw it, got up quickly, and followed him to his office where we stood in the middle of the floor and anxiously scanned the classifieds.

The ad was there. Relief. Everything was set. Our free-world accomplices would be waiting for us at 8 P.M., just as it was getting dark.

Now we were ready for the final countdown. Louis immediately went to the head cook, a trusted friend, and got the keys to the kitchen, which had been locked up since supper time. Carefully he entered the kitchen unobserved and got three large butcher knives, one for each of us. We concealed these beneath our clothing just a few minutes before we were scheduled to be locked into our dormitories along with everyone else. Malcolm and I were in one dorm, and Louis was in the other.

The dorm was hot and stuffy. The air conditioning was poor and the room very crowded—six double bunks in a room fifteen feet square. It seemed as if time would never pass. Looking out one of the room's two windows, I could see the shadows growing long in the humid stillness of the evening. Although it was hot, it was a beautiful summer evening in the Mississippi delta.

In a few minutes now the night watchman would come in to give medicine to those scheduled to get it. Just before eight the door opened, and Malcolm and I were waiting. We flashed the butcher knives on Miller and the trusty with him and told them that they wouldn't be hurt if they co-operated with us. The sight of the large, ugly knives struck immediate terror into both men. They assured us that they would do as we said if we wouldn't hurt them. We then went across the hall, and Miller let Louis out of his dormitory, locking both dorms afterward.

We took Miller's keys out of his pocket and tied up both men with wide adhesive tape that we had secured in advance from the emergency room. So far everything was perfect, smooth. Even the other prisoners in our dorms did not know what had happened. We quickly went to the front hall of the hospital where the intercom system and night watchman's desk were located. This was the most critical and dangerous stage of the whole operation. First we called our trusty friend in off the front tower. Louis had already told him that this would be the night. He came right in as if everything were normal, and we tied him up with tape. Next we called in the only other guard in the front area of the compound. Because it often was difficult to distinguish voices over the intercom, he also came in unsuspecting. This was not unusual. Guards often were summoned in from their posts. When he entered the door, Louis hit him over the head from behind and stunned him momentarily. After he regained his balance and composure, he saw the knives and offered no resistance. Louis and Malcolm then tied him up also.

With everything secure inside the compound and no guards to stop us, the three of us casually walked out the gate, got into the watchman's car, which was in the parking area, and drove off. After driving about a mile down a dirt road that cut through a cotton field, we reached an irrigation creek, but the bridge was washed out. We were more than a mile from the rendezvous point, and we could go no farther by car. But we had known in advance that the bridge was out. We deliberately chose this route in order to make prison officials think that we had hoped to cross the creek and drive off the prison grounds in the watchman's car. When they found the car abandoned they would assume we were afoot in the general vicinity, thus concentrating their search in the wooded areas nearby instead of the highways on which we would be traveling.

As soon as our escape was discovered, the alert would go out to all prison personnel, highway patrolmen, and sheriff's deputies in the area. Prison officials would immediately move out in radio-equipped cars and pickup trucks to preassigned checkpoints in an effort to seal off the area. Since the delta is so flat and has so few trees, men at key positions with binoculars, walkie-talkies, and rifles can command a wide view and often spot escapees running through the fields. Moreover, the prison's pack of bloodhounds would immediately be put on the trail. After years and years of chasing escapees through the same terrain, officials had the art of pursuit down to a science. For this reason, it was absolutely essential that we quickly reach the getaway car and clear the area at once.

Every minute was important now. Success or failure would be determined by how quickly we reached the rendezvous point a mile away. Although it was dusk, the sweltering heat and high humidity were stifling. We waded across the creek, a distance of some thirty feet in water waist high. Because of the soft muddy bottom, it was slow going. Each step would sink us to the ankles in mud.

Running through the fields of young cotton plants, our eyes burned as sweat combined with the dust and began to trickle into our eyes. We had run about a half a mile when we began tiring. My stomach muscles ached. My soggy shoes and trousers felt as if they weighed a hundred pounds. My legs felt weaker and weaker. We were trying to run too fast and couldn't sustain the speed, so we slowed to a more moderate pace: half running, and at times half crawling—to avoid being sighted. It seemed like we would never reach the rendezvous point ahead. Every moment was critical. Life and death were in the balance.

None of us had exercised much in previous months. So the run was extremely tiring. Louis and Malcolm had fallen behind, and I was exhausted. My chest ached and my heart beat wildly. I could hardly lift my legs. Yet somehow I kept going and encouraged the others that we were nearly there. Finally, we sighted the rendezvous point ahead of us.

I didn't see my colleagues anywhere. Hadn't they come —or had they left already? Fear struck my heart. I called out their names. No answer. Again I called. Still no answer. Then suddenly, almost out of nowhere, they emerged from a road in the woods where they had been listening to the monitoring radio in the car.

They were extremely anxious. We had been seen leaving the hospital, and the alert was out, they said. It had been on the air for at least ten minutes. Vehicles were already on the way to seal off the area. Every second was vital. As we piled into the gray Buick Electra convertible, my friends gave Louis and Malcolm each a pistol and me an AR-15 automatic rifle. They both had automatic rifles. A sack of hand grenades was in the front on the floorboard.

We were moving now, heading down the dirt road that would take us to the highway while the prison radio frequency crackled with directives and responses. Everything seemed to be going well. Prison authorities were assuming that we were on foot in the area near where we abandoned the watchman's car. They were concentrating forces in that area while we were moving farther and farther away. Suddenly a pair of headlights appeared in the distance behind us, moving at a high speed. We realized that it was one of the prison vehicles scouting the road, and we sped up. It was gaining on us, probably to try to stop us for a check. So we accelerated even more. It was a dangerous move. To drive on dirt roads is tricky, and if we lost control, the Buick would be a total wreck. Somehow the car held the road, and stirred up so much dust that the prison vehicle was not able to keep up with us and we were able to elude him.

At last we reached U. S. Highway 49 at Drew—five miles south of the prison. From here we proceeded to Greenwood. As we monitored the highway patrol and prison frequencies, we learned that officials were searching the prison area. Before we reached Greenwood, officials had started blocking off roads. So when we came into the city we traveled through residential areas instead of using main thoroughfares. For added security, Malcolm, Louis, and I got out of the car and hid in some brush while our friends checked the highway for roadblocks. About thirty minutes later they returned for us and we drove on to Canton, Mississippi, about seventy miles farther south. Again we repeated this precaution before going on to our hideout. About 2 A.M. we arrived at the hideout, exhausted but safe.

The hideout was an old unused house and barn on a large tract of land situated in a heavily wooded area about two miles from the Jackson Municipal Airport. Because the barn was farthest from the road, we set up operations there. After unloading all our gear, our accomplices left, planning to return the next night with hot food and more supplies. Each of us took turns standing watch while the others slept.

When day broke we prepared some breakfast. We had

ample supplies of army C rations and smokeless cooking fuel. I then scouted out the general area to determine the proximity of roads, houses, water supplies, and so forth. The remainder of the day was uneventful, and when not standing watch, we slept or discussed the next phase of the escape.

The plans were for Louis and Malcolm to go to California and New Orleans, respectively, after the "heat" cooled. I wanted to resume my activities. However, some time would have to pass before I could safely do so. Accordingly, I was thinking of going to South America for a while—at least until the authorities eased off their search. I would spend my time with the old Nazi underground and neo-Nazis who had established an underground network in Argentina and certain other South American countries. When it was safe, I would return to resume my activities.

That night one of our accomplices and his fiancée brought us some hot food. This was an inexcusable breach of security. I protested, but he assured me that she was trustworthy. So there was nothing more I could say, and we got down to the business at hand. We discussed arrangements to get Malcolm and Louis on their way. With them gone I would feel much better and would be able to make more detailed plans for my own situation.

Security appeared to be good. Each news broadcast had less to say about our escape. Soon the investigation and pursuit would phase down. Then we could begin to move out one at a time.

The next day, July 25, 1969, was hot and humid. However, we decided to move out of the barn and set up a tent in some heavy underbrush nearby. This was an added precaution to eliminate the chance of anyone stumbling on us or trapping us in the barn. It was the third day since our escape and I was feeling grubby from not bathing and from lack of sleep. About 7 P.M. Louis came up and relieved me early, and I walked to the tent and fell asleep immediately.

Less than ten minutes had passed when I was awakened by a loud staccato of noises. I was in a daze. Malcolm looked at me in bewilderment. Soon we realized that we were hearing gunfire out near the road where Louis was standing watch—about seventy-five feet away. We took cover behind a fallen tree, and neither of us fired a shot. We were too confused. Out of nowhere a helicopter came down and hovered overhead. Suddenly the shooting stopped. Moments later Roy K. Moore, the FBI chief in Mississippi, called to us on a bull horn, telling us that Louis had been killed and that we were surrounded and should surrender. To flee would have been impossible and resistance would have been fatal. So we agreed to surrender. We came out of our camp with hands high in the air and were at once rushed by at least twenty FBI agents and state police. They ordered us to strip naked, placed us on the ground, and searched us thoroughly. Then we quickly redressed, and our hands were tied behind our backs. We were ordered into FBI cars for the 140-mile trip back to Parchman.

CHAPTER TEN

Our caravan of FBI cars pulled into Parchman late that night. Malcolm and I were both taken to the administration building for interrogation by prison officials, FBI agents, and state investigators. They wanted to know the details of how we had escaped and who had helped us.

Malcolm apparently agreed to answer questions because they talked with him for quite some time. However, I told them I had nothing to say. So I was promptly driven to the maximum security unit by security personnel.

As we approached the well-lit compound with its high barbed fence and forbidding guard towers, I knew that this dismal place would be my home for a long time. The electric gate slowly opened for us to drive into the compound. When the guards took me into the building and the heavy steel door clanged shut behind me with a solemn, final sound, I felt as if I had been sealed in a tomb.

Again I was made to strip naked and was searched. Fresh underwear was given to me, and then I was escorted to the cellblock and locked in a six-foot by nine-foot cell. Here I would spend the next three years of my life.

Since my last stay in the maximum security unit, the number of inmates being held for "safekeeping" had increased considerably. So much, in fact, that there were too many for the extra cells on death row. So prisoners in safekeeping now had a cellblock of their own. Thus I was not taken to death row where I previously had been.

Conditions here were similar to those in death row. We were locked in our cells all the time except for two showers a week. We ate two meals a day, were allowed to buy snacks, and could have radios, books, and magazines. The biggest difference was the noise. It was almost constant. Some prisoners would shout from one end of the cellblock to the other to talk with a friend. Others would play their radios loudly. This wrecked my nerves.

On one occasion several of the guys became provoked with one another because of noise making and began a "noise war" that lasted for a couple of days. Because this "war" affected everyone, even quiet prisoners became involved in retaliation. Some would loudly rattle their cell doors. Others would turn up the volume on their radios. Still others would shout or scream. In various ways, different ones would periodically make loud noise to assure that no one could sleep. At last, probably because of fatigue, they called a truce. However, loud talk and loud radios continued on a sporadic basis throughout my stay.

Noise wasn't the only problem. The heat was terrible. Mississippi summers are hot, and this one was no exception. We had no air conditioning, only a ventilator fan, and although it was better than nothing, it left much to be desired. As the temperature rose during the day, the cells heated up and stayed like an oven until late at night. Often it was so hot that I couldn't get to sleep before 10 or 11 P.M. at the earliest.

One of my great comforts was the visits of my parents. They made the 350-mile trip from Mobile every two weeks to see me, and sometimes my sister and brother would also come. They could only stay two hours, but I always felt encouraged after seeing them. They usually brought me books, magazines, and foodstuffs.

Unfortunately, I was still so selfish that I had no awareness or consideration for their feelings or needs. I was generally moody, frustrated, and irritable. I often would flare up at them about inconsequential things. How sad it was that they faithfully sacrificed to visit and support me only to be met time after time with my selfish, insensitive, abusive behavior. No doubt they often grieved on the long weary ride home because of the way I treated them. Daily mail delivery also was something I really looked forward to. Mail from home and visits were the only close contacts any of us had with the outside world.

As the weeks dragged into months, I occupied myself by reading. Having analyzed the security system, I concluded that escape was not possible. Thus, in order to keep my sanity I read—for relief from the oppressive boredom of prison life.

Little did I know how much the books I read would change me. I began with such books as *Gone With the Wind, Decline and Fall of the Roman Empire* and other well-known volumes. In addition I ordered books by mail dealing with racial and political themes. Some of the main right-wing books that had influenced me in the past were *The Protocols of the Learned Elders of Zion* and *The International Jew* by Henry Ford (the founder of Ford Motor Company). But now I progressed to more sophisticated works such as *The Inequality of Human Races* by Count Arthur de Gobineau, *White America* by Ernest Cox, *Imperium* by Ulick Varange (Francis Parker Yockey), *Mein Kampf* by Adolph Hitler, *Race and Civilization* by Wayne McCloud. I also avidly read *American Mercury Magazine, The Thunderbolt* (NSRP), *The Fiery Cross Magazine* (KKK), and *American Opinion Magazine* (John Birch Society).

Needless to say, reading this type of material served only to reinforce and deepen my racism and anti-Semitism.

After about six months of confinement on the safe-keeping cellblock, I was moved to death row, largely as a result of my parents' requests for a quieter place for me to live. It was much quieter here and much better suited for prolonged incarceration.

After several months of saturating my mind with far-Right and fascist thought, the stimulation of philosophical ideas I encountered in *Imperium* (a book of neo-fascist philosophy that quoted many philosophers) prompted me to begin reading the great philosophers for myself. Little did I know that this course of reading would eventually have a most profound effect upon my life.

I began with Hegel's *Philosophy of History*, which I found intriguing. Oswald Spengler's *Decline of the West* was beyond me in some places but its central thesis spurred my thinking. Yet for some reason I couldn't linger over them long and soon moved on to the writings of Plato, Aristotle, and the Stoics. Here I found a more comfortable and understandable resting place. I was fascinated by Plato's reasoning, his thinking on the immortality of the soul and the ideal state, and his disinterested pursuit of Truth. Also Socrates' view that an unexamined life is not worth living was an inspiration.

Plato and the Stoics helped me recognize how transitory life is and how futile it is to be ruled by what others think of us. We must seek Truth and reality and live accordingly, regardless of what others may think or say.

What Plato and Socrates asserted motivated me to a "disinterested pursuit of Truth" as my most basic attitude toward life. Up to this point I had read only those books that agreed with and supported rightist ideology. I wouldn't read things that were opposed to or incongruent with my views. Thus, I was continually reinforced in my beliefs and never had to weigh them against Truth and reality.

So with a "disinterested" perspective, I began to read *Legacy of Freedom* by George C. Roache. Many passages were important to me, but I was most moved by: "A man willing to judge 'truth' on its merits is the true realist, because he is able to understand that the structure of reality is independent of his own desires. He grasps the fact that the world was created before he arrived and will still be here when he, in his earthly form, has departed."

As I read Plato and Marcus Aurelius, I knew intuitively that they were right. An unexamined life is not worth living (nor an unexamined opinion worth holding). I knew I must seek truth and reality regardless of where that pursuit might take me or what it might cost. If I should find error in views that I had fondly cherished, then I had to abandon them—no matter how sacred they might be.

Clearly these truths changed my whole way of looking at the world. Until now my prejudices, frustrations, emotions, and unconscious needs (recognition, acceptance, adventure) had dictated what was true, right, and good. Indeed, my whole involvement in the radical Right was actually a channel for the outworking and expression of these unconscious problems and needs, just as it is with nearly all other radicals—right, left, or whatever. But now, ideological thinking was abandoned and my intellect took charge and began to rule with a rigorous honesty and cool objectivity. Needless to say, this new way of "seeing" would soon spell the end of my radical ideology and other forms of deception that had bound me through the years.

As I continued to read *Legacy in Freedom*, I saw that the events of history were inextricably bound up with, and reflective of, a highly complex matrix of political, social, cultural, economic, religious, philosophical currents—all of which interacted with one another. Wars and revolutions were not simply part of "Jewish conspiracies." Nor was communism a "Jewish plot." Certainly Jews had been involved in many wars, revolutions, conspiracies, and so forth, but what did that prove? Many more non-Jews than Jews had been involved in these same events. The mere fact of Jewish involvement in an event was not proof of a "Jewish conspiracy." Indeed, I came to see that the radical Right's conspiratorial theory of history (that the ills of society are a result of Jewish conspiracies) was just a simple answer for an extremely complicated set of questions: a simple answer that would readily appeal to a person's prejudices under certain conditions—especially to those with a superficial education or none at all.

Having once had my mind freed to recognize the fallacy of the conspiratorial theory, answers to other questions began to become clear.

Why were persons of Jewish ancestry so often found in positions of power and influence and wealth? If it was true, there were some logical explanations. One of the most basic was that they had been a persecuted minority through the centuries and had come to see the great importance—indeed, the necessity—of gaining wealth and power and favor in order to protect themselves and gain security. That Jews have in some cases acted to protect their individual, community, or national interests was hardly surprising. Could one reasonably expect them to do any less? Surely such reaction to perceived danger was hardly a Jewish conspiracy to dominate the world.

Because Jews have historically felt the need for the security that wealth and power bring, it was only logical that they would place a high premium on education. Through education they could acquire needed skills that would put them in powerful places. That was surely a partial answer to why Jewish people tended to be much better educated than non-Jews and disproportionately visible in the professional, business, and academic worlds.

Jewish people often were raised with a strong religious-cultural heritage; this tends to unify them and to convey that they are a community distinct from non-Jews. This causes many to think in terms of "us" and "them." Such distinctions are exploited with success by anti-Semitic propagandists.

I also began to realize that participation of people with Jewish backgrounds in the Bolshevik Revolution of 1917 in Russia did not constitute proof that "communism was a Jewish plot." For one thing, they were a large and oppressed minority; for another, they were Jewish only in cultural heritage, not in religious belief or practice. Yet when the rightists spoke of Jews, they thought largely in terms of their Jewish religiousness. These Jews, for all intents and purposes, were not Jews at all. Their Jewishness meant absolutely nothing. In fact, many were strongly opposed to the Jewish religion and culture because it presented obstacles to the social leveling plans of Marxism and Leninism. Another point frequently overlooked is that Stalin, a non-Jew, eventually eliminated most of the Jews in the Soviet government during the great purges of the 1930s. Russia had the largest Jewish population of any country in the world during and immediately after the revolution. However, only a minority participated in the overthrow of the czar.

The involvement of persons with Jewish ancestry in the civil rights movement in the United States made sense. Having been the underdog for so long, it should not be surprising that they would sympathize with others similarly oppressed. Many times they had been and were oppressed by the established social structures in which they lived.

I also began to see that Jewish ancestry is a phoney issue—a red herring. For example, much had been made of Karl Marx's Jewish ancestry. But nothing was said of Marx's father converting to Christianity when young Karl was six years old, or that Marx himself was an atheist and held Jews in contempt. The plain truth was that all the communists of Jewish lineage were atheists and had no concern for, or allegiance to, the Jewish religion or culture.

When one considers these and many other facts, it becomes clear that the allegation, "communism is Jewish," is not supported by the weight of evidence. In fact, the evidence indicates just the opposite. In any event, I gradually came to see that the facts did not support the idea of a Jewish conspiracy.

Recognizing the philosophical and moral bankruptcy of radical rightist ideology was a liberating process in my life. It freed my mind. No longer did I have to be careful of what I read "lest some Jewish propaganda inadvertently poison my mind," and no longer did I have to rationalize away truths and realities that didn't fit into my ideology. I was now free to read and study anything I desired and to judge it according to its own merits. Evidence—correspondence with reality—had become the criterion of Truth.

Not long after this, perhaps a month or two, I began reading the Bible again. I can't really say why. Whatever the reason, I started reading in the New Testament, and as I did, the experience was extraordinary. For one thing, I wasn't bored as I always had been. But more important, I was able to understand clearly what I read. The Bible became an open book—a living Word. Charged with meaning, it spoke directly to me. It was almost as if I had been blind all my life and had just received my sight.

The light that lit up within me opened up a whole new world in the Bible. Now for the first time I realized that I was lost. I had always had a mental knowledge of the Truth, to be sure: I knew that all men were sinners and needed to be saved through acceptance of Christ as Savior. But although I knew these truths intellectually and had even made a verbal profession of faith in Christ in

my early teens, I had never had a personal encounter
with the living Christ. I had never really felt the weight
of my own sin. To me it had been a theoretical truth but
never personally felt and experienced. Now it became a
reality for me. I realized that I had never repented of my
sin and surrendered myself to Jesus Christ, living and incarnate. I had merely gone through the forms and said
the right words. I had never been "born again."

One verse of Scripture was especially penetrating:
"What does it profit a man if he gain the whole world and
lose his own soul? And what will a man give in exchange
for his soul?" Yes. This was it. For the previous five years
I had been selling my soul to gain the world. Although I
thought I was motivated by dedication to my ideals, in
truth I used my activities to receive recognition, acceptance, and approval from my peers. In other words, my activities provided me with a sense of worth. They fed my
ego.

As the full impact of all this began to break upon me, I
was overcome with a sense of my sinfulness—not just for
prejudice, hatred, and political violence, but for my
whole life-style. All my life I had been living for myself—
what pleased me, made me feel good, made me look good
to others. The feelings, needs, desires of other people
were always secondary to what I wanted. Indeed, the
whole world revolved around me and this showed itself in
the outward sins of my life.

As I came to see myself as I really was—as God saw me
—I was crushed, and I wept bitterly. How hideous and
wretched I was. Then, seeing my need so clearly and
knowing there was only One who could meet it, I gave
myself to the Lord Jesus Christ as fully as I knew how. In
that moment a tremendous weight was lifted from me,
and I began to feel peace at last.

CHAPTER ELEVEN

"Once I was blind, but now I see," said a man whom Jesus healed. So it is with all who truly encounter Jesus Christ; for having once met Him, it is impossible ever to be the same again. Certainly that is true for me.

In my early teens I had made a profession of faith, been baptized, and had become a member of a church. But my relationship to the Lord and my behavior remained the same—even though I thought I would go to heaven when I died. I was like so many good people in churches who think that they are religious although they do not know Jesus Christ personally. This is true throughout the United States, but it is particularly prevalent in those areas where religion has been a strong part of the culture, and people have an outward form of good behavior and religion.

But to be a church member, believe right doctrine, or be impeccably moral and do good works are not the essence of life with God. These are all important and good, but one can have all of these qualities and still not know the risen Christ. Jesus said that eternal life consists in knowing God personally. When that happens one's life is changed.

That is what happened to me. Now I had a relationship with Jesus that brought immediate and drastic changes in my life. I began to pray and to read the Bible for hours on end—and I loved both. Most notably, I no longer wanted to be the person I once was; rather I wanted to be the kind of person God wanted me to be. I wanted to be free from all sin, and live close to God. When I did yield to temptation, I was sorry.

This was an important time for me, and fortunately Glenn Howell played a vital part in my life during these formative days. A recent graduate of Asbury Theological Seminary in Kentucky, he had just joined the prison staff as a chaplain when the head chaplain brought Glenn to the maximum security unit to meet the men.

Because of my new relationship with Jesus, I was eager to read anything dealing with the Lord, and I asked Glenn if he had any books I might read. So he began to bring me books that would help me understand my faith. One of the books he brought me was written by Samuel Craig, a Presbyterian theologian. It set forth a clear explanation of the basic truths of Scripture and gave me a good grasp of common departures from Truth. Through the quotations and influences cited in that book I became aware of a larger body of Presbyterian theology and was soon ordering works that interested me.

I had been reading such classics as *The Imitation of Christ* by Thomas à Kempis; *Screwtape Letters, Mere Christianity*, and *Miracles* by C. S. Lewis; and some novels of Taylor Caldwell. But now I began to pursue formal theology such as Berkhof's *Systematic Theology*, the works of B. B. Warfield, and books on apologetics by Cornelius Van til, E. J. Carnell, Floyd Hamilton, and others.

As my interest in theology grew, I developed a lively and regular correspondence with Dr. Morton Smith, at that time president of the Reformed Theological Seminary in Jackson. Dr. Smith gave me guidance and counsel and provided other good books, such as Calvin's *Institutes*, Hodges' *Systematic Theology*, and others.

So in addition to my daily Bible reading and prayers, I spent hours each day exploring not only theology and apologetics, but the relationship of Jesus Christ to science, philosophy, and other disciplines of study. Such reading helped me develop a clear grasp of faith, of Truth, and of the major issues of contemporary theology.

These two years of study in theology were a time of immense intellectual growth, but it was also a time of increasing spiritual "dryness." The reason was simple: I allowed knowledge about God to overshadow my personal relationship with Him. There's a big difference. It's easy to get so wrapped up in study about God and the Scripture that one neglects to develop his or her personal relationship with Him. Strangely enough, I find that this seems to be a special danger that seminary students and faculty, pastors and scholars, and workers have to guard against. How sad it is to see people whose intellectual lives have overshadowed their devotional life and rendered them dry and almost lifeless, or, even worse, dogmatic and legalistic. In this, as in all other areas of life, balance is crucial. An increasing knowledge of God's truth should always go hand in hand with a deepening intimacy with Him.

One day, in the midst of all these studies, I had a rather unusual visitor—the Reverend Ken Dean of Jackson, head of the Mississippi Council on Human Relations. He was a prominent liberal and civil rights advocate in the state who had been interested in my case from the beginning. He felt that I had been the victim of a trap and, along with his wife, Mary, had become good friends with my mother and father.

Liberal in his theology as well as his politics, Ken was the last person with whom I was interested in developing a friendship. Obviously I was suspicious of his motives

and was guarded in what I said. However, I found that
he was a rather nice person. Our conversation that day
ranged over many topics, dealing with nothing in particular. Its only significance was that it was a beginning. I
had always intensely hated liberals and civil rights
workers, but now for the first time I was getting to know
one personally—and found myself liking him.

As the months passed, Ken and I kept in touch by mail
—even after he moved to New York for graduate studies
at Colgate Divinity School. In one of his letters while at
Colgate, he said that he and Mary had decided they
would like to help me financially if I should want to return to college after I was released.

Gradually I came to see him as a very complex person
with whom I disagreed on political theory and theology,
but one who was genuinely concerned about my welfare.

About this time another relationship began developing
with an equally unlikely person—Joyce Watts, the wife of
FBI Agent Frank Watts. After word was circulated that I
had met Jesus Christ, Frank and his partner, Jack Rucker,
had come to the prison to see me.

They had been sent by J. Edgar Hoover, who thought I
was probably trying to use "religion" as a means of con-
ning someone and getting an opportunity to escape.
Frank and Jack talked with me for a while and then I
shared what had happened to me. They listened with intense interest because, as they later told me, they had
never seen such a change in a person. But then came a
tough question: "Now that you really know Christ, don't
you think it is your duty to testify against your associates
and put them behind bars? After all, they are dangerous
people and have broken the laws. For the good of society
they need to be locked up." My response probably
seemed like a cop-out. I told them that I could think of
nothing more contemptible than a person who would be-
tray his friends or his principles for personal advantage.

As I saw it, the crimes I committed with these people were done out of a common commitment and mutual trust. It would be wrong, I reasoned, to testify against them now—especially because they were no longer engaged in violence. It would seem to everyone that my newfound relationship with Christ was just a con game to get out of prison by becoming "righteous" and testifying against my former associates. That would dishonor Jesus.

When Frank returned home and told his wife of the changes in my life, she decided to write me a letter and send me some books. Joyce was active in prayer groups and Bible studies and had recently come into a deeper relationship with Christ. She was quite an encouragement to me. So was Frank, who also came into a deeper walk with God not long after his wife. Through the years he and I became very close friends, and he did much to help me—often at the expense of his social and professional reputation. And had it not been for his standing up for me over the years that followed, I would probably still be in prison.

I had known the Lord for a year and had been in the maximum security unit for two years when E. R. Moody, the sergeant in charge of the unit, asked me if I would like to get out of my cell for a few hours a day to do clerical work for him in the office. He had observed me for a year and saw the changes God had made in my life. So he decided to do all he could to help me. It would be an opportunity to prove myself, he said, and might eventually get me out of the maximum security unit into the general prison population. Much later I learned that Sergeant Moody had gone to the superintendent and put his job on the line in order to get permission to offer me this job.

I worked for Sergeant Moody a full year, doing the best job I possibly could, and we became good friends.

There were to be other changes in my prison status. Several of them came in the year 1972. A new governor,

Bill Waller, took office in January and shortly thereafter appointed a new superintendent at the state penitentiary. John Collier, the new appointee, was a prominent plantation owner from the delta and a dedicated follower of Christ. The choice of a plantation owner instead of a penologist may seem a bit odd at first, but when one considers that Parchman was actually a sixteen-thousand-acre farm operated with inmate labor, it becomes understandable.

One day in the spring of 1972, Collier made an inspection tour of the maximum security unit. I was working in the office while he went through the cellblocks meeting the men. So I didn't have a chance to see him just then. However, he saw my cell—cluttered as it was with stacks of religious books and literature—and wanted to know who I was. After completing his inspection he came into the office and saw some more of my books scattered around where I was working.

He courteously introduced himself and asked if the books were mine. He then said, "Do you know the Lord?" I told him I did, and after a very brief conversation, he left.

During the next couple of months I saw Collier two or three times and then only briefly. But the chief of security, staff psychologist, and the four chaplains regularly made rounds at the maximum security unit, and I had gotten to know them all quite well. So all of these men went to bat for me in May when my new supervisor, Sergeant Pat Mooney, recommended that I be given "trusty" status. The classification committee unanimously approved the recommendation, and Mr. Collier concurred.

Changes in my situation soon became more rapid. These same friends felt that the time had come for me to be released from the maximum security unit altogether, and within two months they brought the matter up with Collier who had me transferred to a garage apartment in back of his home there on the prison grounds. He assigned me to work as a clerk in the chaplain's office— located in the administration building nearby.

For someone just out of maximum security, this kind of move wasn't just unusual or extraordinary—it was absolutely unheard of. Never before had anything like this been done.

There were many skeptics on the prison staff who were uneasy at seeing me in the halls of the administration building each day. They thought Collier was naïve if not stupid—and that I had conned him with "jail house religion." Some—and I can certainly understand their point of view—were predicting that I would escape within the week because there were no guards or locked doors to prevent my leaving the administration building or garage apartment. As I went about my daily work in the chaplain's office, the weeks grew into months and quite a few of the doubters realized that I had, indeed, been changed. Nonetheless, some wouldn't be convinced. They no doubt still view my conversion as a gimmick for freedom.

I sought to be diligent in my duties in the chaplain's office and this brought to light a talent for administrative work, especially writing and research. As a result, various members of the executive staff gave me special assignments from time to time. These ranged from doing research projects on needed prison programs to writing reports and even drafting sample legislation. In this way I was able to make a contribution toward improving prison conditions and programs for the inmates.

In addition to my daily clerical duties in the chaplain's office, I often accompanied the chaplains on their rounds to the camps, taught regular Bible studies, and went with the chaplain on speaking engagements in the free world.

A rather unusual and interesting sidelight to this phase of my time at Parchman was the friendships that developed. Collier, his wife, and children were all very kind to me and we soon became friends. The same was true of Assistant Superintendent Jack Byars and his wife; Associate Superintendent Liberty Cash; and Farm Manager Ed McBride and his wife, who was the prison receptionist. The skeptics, of course, said that I had just conned these people and was using them until I could escape. But nothing could have been further from the truth. The simple fact was that God had given me favor with them and had established genuine friendships—which have continued to the present day.

In late fall of 1972 Collier resigned and was followed by Bill Hollowell, a former sheriff and highway patrolman. Hollowell, who was quite security conscious, took a dim view of my living at the superintendent's house—which had no security at all. Consequently, I was assigned to work and live at the pre-release center.

Although it was a minimum-security honor camp without fences or guards, it did have round-the-clock supervisory personnel. It was a facility where parolees were sent three weeks prior to release. There they received counseling and instruction designed to ease the transition from prison to free society.

Unlike an ordinary camp, pre-release was modeled more on the lines of a college dormitory, and a deliberate effort was made to create as normal an environment as possible. A large, well-furnished, and carpeted lounge area opened into a modern cafeteria, forming the center of the building. On either side was a wing. The left housed an open dormitory with modern double bunk beds, chest of drawers, and curtains. The right contained a classroom and a suite of offices housing the Division of Vocational Rehabilitation (DVR).

My new assignment consisted of assisting the rehabilitation staff of four counselors and their secretaries. My duties initially were few: making coffee twice a day, keeping the staff lounge clean, making copies on the

Xerox machine, and so forth. However, I was soon asked
to begin teaching courses to the parolees. One course,
Success Through a Positive Mental Attitude, was a moti-
vational course; another, World of Work, centered on
employer-employee relations, and the other was a driver's
education course. I taught these courses for four years.

Within a year the chaplain's department moved its
offices to the pre-release center, and my duties were ex-
panded to include serving once again as clerk for the department. This enabled me to spend more time with
Glenn Howell. His practical wisdom and encouragement
were of inestimable value in my spiritual growth, and our
friendship really grew.

Several months after I had moved to the pre-release
center the Reverend Ken Dean and I began com-
municating more frequently. One of the major themes of
Ken's theology in those days was reconciliation—of persons and groups who were racially or politically alienated
from one another. It was his desire to see me reconciled
with my enemies, and they with me. To this end he
suggested the possibility of my meeting with Alvin
Binder.

Binder was a prominent attorney in Mississippi and
leader of the state's Jewish community. When the Klan
began its terror campaign against the Jews, he took a year
from his lucrative law practice to help stop it. A tough-
minded, highly competent man, he had played a crucial
role, along with the FBI, in breaking up the Klan.

I told Ken that I would be glad to meet with Binder if
he could arrange it with prison officials. He did, and a few
weeks later the two men came to the prison.

It was somewhat tense at first. Binder, trial lawyer that
he is, fired questions at me in rapid fashion—trying to see
if I was going to lie or evade him or otherwise try to
deceive him. I answered him truthfully and directly, and
he began to realize that I was not playing a game. When

he left that afternoon, not only had there been a reconciliation, but the foundation had been laid for what would be a solid friendship.

Reconciliation continued when I met and became good friends with several other very unlikely people. The most notable, perhaps, was Douglass Baker. Doug was a black civil rights lawyer who was serving a short term at Parchman for embezzlement. An intelligent, cultured, and articulate man, Doug was outspoken in his racial and political beliefs. Yet strange and unlikely as it was, he and I became good friends and entertained high regard for one another. Shortly after Doug was released, he met Jesus Christ and is now a changed man.

Two other guys with whom I developed good friendships were Vic Nance and Bill Rusk, both white. Before his incarceration Vic, a college student, had been a longhaired hippie drug user. While in Parchman he came to know Christ, and the two of us became close brothers, although occasionally we were antagonistic to one another. After he was released from Parchman, Vic went on to college, then into full-time prison ministry. Bill, on the other hand, was a dedicated radical, and told me he had once been a member of the leftist Students for a Democratic Society (SDS). Strangely, Bill and I also became good friends. He was a highly intelligent, mild-mannered guy, and I respected and liked him very much.

I had been reconciled with Frank Watts of the FBI; then Ken Dean, the liberal civil rights leader; Al Binder, the Jewish leader; Doug Baker, militant civil rights lawyer; Vic Nance, the hippie drug user; and Bill Rusk, an activist on the radical Left. What a list of friends for a former right-wing terrorist. Not only is God in the business of reconciliation, but He has a sense of humor as well.

Reconciliation wasn't the only thing God was doing in

my life during these years. In fact, it wasn't even one of the major things.

I was introduced to a number of unusual believers in my life who were to have a profound influence on my spiritual growth.

One of these was Dr. Wilson Benton, minister of the First Presbyterian Church of nearby Cleveland, Mississippi. Wilson, who was about my age, had received his Ph.D. in systematic theology from Edinburgh University, Scotland, and was a master teacher and effective counselor. But more than this, he loved God. He came to the prison often, and we were good friends.

Another was the Reverend Jack Moore, the pastor of First Baptist Church in nearby Rulville, Mississippi. Young and dynamic, Jack also was an unusually gifted preacher, teacher, and counselor. He, too, was a frequent visitor, and his passionate love for God was a great example to me—and the basis of a deep brotherly love.

The Reverend Cecil Pumphrey, a Baptist pastor whose ministry reached into Arkansas and Tennessee, was yet another one of those whom God used greatly in my life. Cecil was a most extraordinary man. Humble, yet strong and wise, he had an unusual closeness with God and was very sensitive to the Holy Spirit. He experienced God's guidance and provision on a daily basis and in ways that few people know. He could see right into your heart, discern your problems and needs, and minister to them in a way that would bring encouragement and strength.

It was through Cecil that I met James E. Rankin, administrative assistant to Senator John Stennis and director of the senator's office in Jackson, Mississippi. Like Cecil, James was deeply committed to God and very sensitive to the voice of the Lord. He and I also became close brothers.

These persons were vital in my spiritual growth, but God used the chaplain's secretary, Wendy Hatcher, more

than anyone else in my life. The wife of a prominent
Cleveland, Mississippi, attorney, Wendy had been a social-
ite in Mississippi delta society. Then after seeing the
vanity and emptiness of the "good life," she had a life-
changing encounter with Jesus Christ. From that day she
was a different person—a totally committed disciple of
Christ. Because of this she took a position at Parchman.
She believed that the Lord had provided her with an opportunity for ministry among the women inmates.

Unlike Wilson, Jack, Cecil, and James, Wendy was
around me on a daily basis. Seldom did a day pass without our discussing the Bible and the Christian life, and
she was always bringing me religous books and tapes. It
was through these—especially the books of Dr. Martin
Lloyd-Jones and the taped sermons of Dr. Albert Martin—
that I began to go really deeper into Christ. In a very real
sense, she formed a bridge between me and the believers
in the free world. More importantly, often it fell her lot to
pray and counsel me through times of doubt, confusion,
and despair. On more than one occasion I fell prey to
doubting my salvation and once was almost sure I was
not really saved. During times such as these, Wendy
would alert my friends throughout the state to pray for
me, and she would try to minister in whatever way she
could.

Then there were others, too many to mention in detail—
Frank Watts who did so much to help me through the
years; Phil Shurden and his cousin Mike, sons of prosper-
ous delta planters who visited me often; Steve Hale, an
athlete and student at Delta State University; David
Daves and Jim Carson who ran a coffee house in Cleveland; Danny Lynchard, a young Baptist minister; Walter
Herbison and Helen Yurkow, prominent citizens in Cleveland; Gene Powell, a pilot; Jerrel Davis, a Buick dealer
in Meridian, and his wife, Norma.

All these and more were faithful in visiting and praying

for me. Through them God encouraged and strengthened me and enabled me to endure those years. These were the true heroes of my story and whatever ministry I have shall always rest on the foundation God built into me through them.

Late in the spring of 1976 I met a man who was to have a far greater effect on my life than either of us might have guessed. Dr. Leighton Ford, an evangelist with the Billy Graham Evangelistic Association, held a service at the prison one day as part of a delta-wide Reachout crusade centered in Cleveland. The First Presbyterian Church was one of the sponsoring churches, and some of my friends in Cleveland urged Leighton to meet me. When he came to the prison to preach, we had a brief talk—the beginning of what grew to be a great friendship. When Leighton returned to Cleveland he suggested to my minister, Wilson Benton, that it would be good for me to attend Chuck Colson's prison discipleship program in Washington, D.C. The church volunteered to provide any expense involved, and Leighton undertook to contact Colson. Colson promptly sent a letter to prison officials inviting me to Washington for the two-week program. This was a highly unusual request, especially for someone as politically controversial as I was. The warden and staff were very supportive, but something of this nature—leaving the state for two weeks unescorted—had to be personally approved by the governor. In view of who I was, the odds were a million to one against it. But God had His hand in the whole affair, and through a set of circumstances that can only be described as miraculous, Governor Cliff Finch gave his approval.

So I went to Washington. During my two weeks there I got to know a dozen other inmates—all from federal prisons. It was a time of close fellowship, solid teaching, and spiritual growth. It was also the beginning of some very rewarding friendships with three special men: Chuck Colson, Harold Hughes, and Dr. Richard Halverson.

The high point of the conference came at a banquet the night before we left. This banquet, at the Fellowship House in the Embassy Row section of Washington, was a commencement service for the men in the discipleship group.

I was in the kitchen talking with someone when Chuck Colson came in and told me he wanted to introduce me to Eldridge Cleaver, former head of the Black Panther Party —the black equivalent of the KKK. I had already heard of Eldridge's conversion, so I was eager to meet him. But as we were going out to the living room I asked Chuck rather facetiously, "Are you sure this guy's saved?" Quite amused, he assured me there was nothing to worry about.

A moment later I found myself shaking hands with a man whom I would have bitterly hated several years before, but for whom I now felt only love and acceptance as a brother in Christ.

Later that night as we were eating supper around a table that included Harold Hughes, a liberal Democrat, and Chuck Colson, a conservative Republican, Eldridge and I rose to share brief reflections with those present.

Little did I realize at the time the magnitude of what God was doing. Nonetheless, God was again working out one of His favorite themes—reconciliation through the power of the risen Christ.

Truly, Jesus lives, and He is Lord.

CHAPTER TWELVE

In late summer of 1974 I told the Reverend Ken Dean of Superintendent Bill Hollowell's supportive attitude toward my desire to be released to attend college. Hollowell said that at the proper time he would present the matter to the governor who had to give final approval. Wanting to help in every possible way, Ken talked with Hollowell and his close friend, Lt. Gov. William Winter. He also spoke with key white liberals and leaders of the black community to assure them of my changed life. It was Hollowell's thinking, and Ken's as well, that the leaders of the black community and the Jewish community should be agreeable to my release. Through Ken's indefatigable efforts this was accomplished.

Henry Barmettler, the staff psychologist, took a major part in all the arrangements for my admission to college. He had given me a thorough psychological evaluation and was eager to see me released. He even drove me to Jackson to take the Scholastic Aptitude Test, a standard college admission test. Henry, along with Asst. Supt. Liberty Cash, wrote letters of recommendation to the colleges where I was making application.

Through the efforts of Ken and Henry I was eventually admitted to Rutgers College in New Jersey, Duke University in North Carolina, and Earlham College in Indiana.

Acceptance by such schools as these would certainly be helpful in my bid for release.

All arrangements had now been completed. I had made extremely high SAT scores. I had been accepted by three excellent schools. I was recommended by the prison psychologist and executive staff. My former political enemies had agreed to my release, and even the lieutenant governor was ready to support it publicly.

But when the proposal was finally broached to the governor, the answer was negative. In a televised news conference the governor said that while I had made considerable progress during my years in Parchman, he didn't feel it was time for me to be released.

To say that I was disappointed would be an understatement. I was utterly dejected. It seemed that there was no hope left for an early release. If this effort failed, as strong as it was, no effort would succeed. I would be at Parchman twenty more years. For several days I had to fight strong feelings of bitterness, resentment, and depression. Gradually God showed me a simple but important Truth. Those works which originate in the wisdom and strength of our human nature are not God's works. They are our own, and we cannot expect His blessings upon them. "My ways are not your ways. Neither are my thoughts your thoughts," says the Lord. His works are not accomplished by might nor by power, but by His Spirit.

I had made my plans and had expected the Lord to prosper them. But He didn't cooperate. It wasn't His time for me to be released and neither was this His way to go about it.

As I prayed through this crisis, God impressed upon me in a clear, unmistakable way that He would set me free in His time and His way, and that I must make no further efforts or plans to bring it about in my own strength.

In the spring of 1976, nearly two years later, changes in state law made me eligible for the work-release program.

This change had come as a result of a federal court order to reduce overcrowded conditions. The inmate population was 2,600 and rising, far above the 1,900 maximum capacity.

This meant that I could possibly be released from Parchman about Christmas time of 1976. Two of the counselors, Tommy Worthey and Steve Lawhon, began to do the early groundwork, and I hadn't suggested it to them. I had to be given a thorough psychological evaluation by the staff psychologist and appear before the prison classification committee for their approval.

Then there was the matter of securing a job and sponsor. Because many of my closest friends were in Cleveland, Mississippi, only twenty-five miles away, I naturally wanted to go there. In order for me to locate there it was necessary for the county sheriff and chief circuit judge to give their approval. But my friends there were leaders of the community. So their recommendations would assure my being approved. I prayed, however, that if this wasn't where God wanted me, He would shut the door. And shut the door He did. The sheriff refused to approve my coming.

At this point Chaplain Glenn Howell and Ed McBride, who was now a top administrator, began to get more involved in helping me find a place to settle. Because I also had some friends in Tupelo, Mississippi, I decided to apply there. Again I prayed that God would shut this door as well if it weren't His place for me. Again, officials refused to accept me.

In view of my notoriety, it was going to be difficult, I realized, for a sheriff and judge to approve my living in their jurisdiction.

For one thing I was at one time labeled by the press and federal and state authorities as the most dangerous man in Mississippi. More importantly, I had shot a patrolman—an extremely serious offense in its own right. So, if most of the local citizenry didn't protest the possibility of my coming to a community, at least the Jews or the local authorities would.

On the day I learned of my rejection by Tupelo, I was scheduled to speak to a class of law-enforcement students from the University of Mississippi. Tour groups regularly visited the pre-release center. They would view the facilities, eat lunch in the modern cafeteria, and often talk with some of the inmates there. Many times I would be called on by the tour guide, Mrs. Jean McBride, to address the group and answer questions.

When I completed my talk, Mrs. McBride mentioned to the group that because of political matters I was having trouble finding a county to accept me on work release. At the mention of this, Dr. Chester Quarles, the professor of the class on the tour, became interested in helping me. More than anything else, I wanted to resume my college studies. So Dr. Quarles, who was director of the university's law-enforcement program, said he would check on the possibility of my being admitted to the university. He also said he would intercede on my behalf with the circuit judge, district attorney, sheriff, and chief of police in Oxford where the university is located—and what's more, that he would try to find me a part-time job.

This was tremendous—absolutely tremendous! But I had let my hopes build up twice and had been disappointed. I couldn't get totally enthused about this possibility because the same thing might well happen again. I was optimistic—but guardedly so.

Step by step everything fell into place. My application for admission was accepted. State and federal grants were offered to me. Community officials gave their approval, and a part-time job (at night) became available. As all these things were developing, the prison bureaucracy was completing my paperwork.

By Monday, December 6, 1976, everything had been

completed except the report of the parole officer in Oxford who had to investigate the job, sponsor, and living plans. Once this was in, Warden John Watkins and Dr. Allen Ault, the state commissioner of corrections, would review my case for approval or disapproval. Disapproval at any level would prevent my release.

Months earlier a number of my close friends had written the governor asking that my sentence be reduced so I could be eligible for release. These requests were forwarded by the governor's office to the parole board for evaluation and recommendation. After looking into the matter at length and weighing the pros and cons, the parole board recommended that no clemency be granted at that time. This report was sent to the governor's office just a few days before I was to be considered for the work-release program.

On December 8, Dr. Ault was scheduled to be at the prison to review inmate records for possible release. This would be a good time for me to be considered because a federal court order called for a reduction of the prison population by the end of December. If Dr. Ault could somehow interview me instead of merely reviewing my record, then my chances would be enhanced even more.

But my papers were still incomplete. The parole officer at Oxford hadn't yet made the routine investigation of my job, employer, and housing arrangements. At this point God used my long-time friend, Ed McBride. Ed phoned the parole officer that morning and asked him to complete the investigation before noon. Ed, who was a pilot, then flew his plane to Oxford, ninety miles away, met the parole officer at the airport, and got the papers, and returned to Parchman. Everything was then set.

Through the efforts of Ed and his wife, Jean, Chaplain Glenn Howell, and Carole Arnold, the warden's secretary, Dr. Ault and Mr. Watkins agreed to interview me that afternoon.

About 1 P.M. I was advised to get ready to go to the warden's office. This was, after all, going to be the big day for me. Today I would find out once and for all whether I had any chance of being released soon or would be locked up for several more years.

I immediately asked Wendy to notify some of my key friends to be in prayer. Then Wendy and I began to pray. In the midst of the excitement and tension, I felt a deep peace and was able to pray with an honest heart that God's perfect will would prevail—even if that meant my being turned down. During those two hours of waiting to be taken to the warden's office, I gained a deeper appreciation of Christ's struggle in the Garden of Gethsemane. I wanted very much to be free, but more than that or anything else, I wanted my Father's perfect will—even if it meant spending the rest of my life in prison. It was hard to pray that way, but through His grace I was able to say, "Not my will, but Yours, be done."

At length the guards came and drove me from the pre-release center to the administration building, a distance of about six miles. What a strange feeling it was as I looked out across the brown fields to realize that the long-awaited day might have finally come.

We pulled up at the administration building and entered the warden's outer office. In a few moments a tall, neatly dressed man in his late forties came out and introduced himself as John Watkins, the warden. Inviting me into his office, he introduced me to Dr. Allen Ault. Watkins, a well-educated man with a forceful personality, began asking me questions while Dr. Ault sat quietly to the side. The questions were fast and varied; sometimes they would follow a definite line of thinking and other times be unrelated.

He asked about my family relations with Mother and Father and about my home life. Then he switched abruptly to my former ideological beliefs. He wanted to know what they were and why I once believed them. He asked what had made me change. Then he asked for my views on the contemporary social and political scene. My plans interested him greatly, and he probed for details.

This continued for about half an hour, during which he backtracked several times. I felt as if I were being interrogated by a skilled intelligence officer. At times he would question me as a psychologist, at times as a sociologist, yet always as a skeptic.

Suddenly the questioning was completed. The decision had been made. Watkins said that he had been around prisons too long to have any confidence at all in my "Christianity," and that he would not release me on the strength of my religion, which, he said, I would discard the day I got out. "No, I'm not going to release you because of your religion, because I don't think it's worth five cents. But I do believe you have changed and deserve a chance to make something of yourself. That's why I'm going to release you."

As he spoke those words I felt a deep relief and a surge of exhilaration and joy welling up. There would be no long suspenseful wait. Dr. Ault then asked, "Will Monday be soon enough to leave?" "Yes, sir," I said, "Monday will be just fine." In my heart I would have liked to have left the next day, but after all these years, five more days wouldn't make that much difference.

Somehow I managed to express my appreciation and make a graceful exit. As I left the office, friends on the staff who had been sweating out the interview came up to learn the verdict. When I told them the news, they were overjoyed—and some, in fact, were more excited than I was.

Chaplain Glenn Howell drove me back to the pre-release center. Ironically this dear brother who had come to Parchman only weeks after my conversion and had encouraged and supported me all these years would himself be leaving in just a few short months. Truly, God had brought him to Parchman to be with me and help me during the prison years. How grateful I am for Glenn's Wesleyan influence, which tempered my rigid dogmatism. What a loving, all-wise God we serve.

Sunday, December 12, Glenn gave a going-away party for me at his home. There on the prison grounds my friends from around Mississippi came to see me for the last time at Parchman. It was an emotional time for all of us—a time of joy and gratitude in remembering God's past blessings and in anticipating the future.

On a bright, clear Monday morning, December 13, 1976, at about 8:30 A.M., a prison station wagon arrived at the pre-release center where I had spent the last three years. I was packed and ready to leave. I said good-by to my fellow inmates who had to remain behind, but it was difficult to believe that I was leaving the center for the last time. When we arrived at the identification office, I found that it had been moved into a new, modern facility that very morning. Nonetheless, Sergeant Miller, who admitted me to Parchman eight years previously, was still in charge. He was genuinely glad to see me getting out, and he wished me well. I was then driven down guard row to the administration building where Dr. Quarles and his wife had come to pick me up and take me to Oxford. As we rode down guard row, colorful Christmas decorations were in the windows of the houses, just as they were that December day eight years ago when I had first arrived. Now I could feel the joy of Christmas. The bleak despair had finally passed.

There had been many changes at Parchman in those years, and many changes in the world, yet to me the greatest change was what Christ had done in my life. And now it was time for me to return to the world to share the love and mercy of Him who had truly made me free.

AFTERWORD

As this book is released for publication, I sincerely hope
that its true message, the greatness of God's love and
mercy, will not be obscured by secondary issues.

Right-wing radicals may, of course, focus on ideology
and dismiss the entire story with the charge that it is a lie
or trick of the communist-Jewish conspiracy and allege
that I have obviously been bribed and brainwashed by
the Jews or by the FBI. Any attempt to answer such a
charge probably would be pointless.

Because my case has been so publicized, the mass
media probably will focus on the lack of detail concerning controversial matters—especially on those issues
raised by Jack Nelson of the *Los Angeles Times*. Such
digression, however, would have distracted from the
book's theme and purpose, the love and mercy of the
Lord for a wretched sinner.

Much has been made of the FBI's involvement in my
case. In a special investigative report published by the
Los Angeles Times, Jack Nelson indicated that the FBI
used $80,000 in reward money raised by the Jewish com-
munity to induce the two informants, Wayne and Raymond Roberts, to lure me into a trap. However, the truth
is that Meyer Davidson had become a high-priority target
in my mind before the Roberts brothers became FBI in-

formants. So the FBI did not lure us into doing something we had no intention of doing.

As I have said elsewhere, if it hadn't been for the FBI's intelligence program there would have been ten times as much violence by right-wing radicals. Fear of informers, sophisticated listening devices, phone taps, and other surveillance procedures promoted disunity, dissension, distrust, suspicion, and paranoia that prevented us from planning and executing many acts of violence. Those who have reservations about the use of an FBI intelligence program directed toward radical groups might do well to put themselves in the position of the potential victim. Liberals and conservatives alike should realize that their lives may one day depend on such a program—just as Meyer Davidson's did.

Those who have social concerns about law enforcement and practices may tend to focus on the role of the FBI and the actions of the Meridian police. But my purpose has not been to defend myself, assign guilt to others, or discredit law enforcement. Rather, I have attempted to tell a story in which these events were integral. Whether or not the Meridian police gave me proper warning before opening fire is a matter about which we have always differed. But this difference of opinion is no longer relevant to me. Policemen are human—just like the rest of us. These particular men were under great pressure to stop a dangerous, terrorist organization that would certainly have claimed innocent lives had it been allowed to continue unopposed. Moreover, those of us whom the police expected to be on the bombing mission were reported to be armed with submachine guns and hand grenades. This was true. So I can understand how the Meridian police could not afford to take any chances.

The other point that may concern a few persons is what happened when the police found me unarmed and semiconscious in the bushes—after the car chase and shoot-out. That they opened fire on me at that point cannot be justified, but it can be understood. I had just shot a policeman, and he was nearly dead, lying in the street a hundred feet away from where I was.

For one to focus on these issues would be a great misfortune. Obviously nothing short of supernatural interaction was at work—time after time. By God's grace I was protected despite my vile behavior. It was a miracle:

—That I survived the initial barrage of gunfire at the Davidson house. Not knowing where the shots were coming from I ran back to my car, right into the fire of half a dozen sharpshooters who were on the other side of the street about thirty feet away.

—That I wasn't blown up when I dropped the bomb. Army demolition experts said that the dynamite that had been hit by initial gunfire was old, very sensitive to shock, and extremely dangerous. The impact of the buckshot hitting the dynamite and of its falling to the ground were enough to detonate it.

—That I survived the ensuing high-speed chase during which round after round of gunfire was pumped into my car.

—That Patrolman Hatcher survived three machine-gun bullets in the chest, one of which was in his heart.

—That I wasn't killed by any one of the four shotgun blasts that were fired at almost point-blank range by the police.

—That I fully recovered from injuries that caused doctors to give me no more than forty-five minutes to live.

—That I was not on guard when law-enforcement officials attacked our hideaway after our escape from prison. The accomplice who was killed relieved me early. I should have been where he was when the FBI closed in. If I had been, I would have been killed instead of him.

—That I was transferred out of the maximum security unit, especially in view of the fact that the governor of

Mississippi and the FBI were determined that I remain there for the duration of my sentence.

—That I was finally released from prison by a man who had never met me, had no confidence in my conversion, and could see only my evil behavior in the prison files. All the preparations fell into place perfectly.

These events, to name only a few, are the real points on which the reader should focus. They demonstrate that more than coincidence or luck or human effort was involved. Truly the living Christ was active to redeem me and work out His plan for my life.

With St. Paul I can only say:

> I thank Christ Jesus our Lord, who has strengthened me, because He considered me faithful, putting me into service; even though I was formerly a blasphemer and a persecutor and a violent aggressor. And yet I was shown mercy because I acted ignorantly in unbelief; and the grace of our Lord was more than abundant with the faith and love which are found in Christ Jesus. It is a trustworthy statement, deserving full acceptance, that Christ Jesus came into the world to save sinners among whom I am foremost of all. And yet for this reason I found mercy, in order that in me as the foremost Christ Jesus might demonstrate His perfect patience, as an example for those who would believe in Him for eternal life.
>
> I Timothy 1:12–16

EPILOGUE

by Harold E. Hughes

The amazing transforming power of Jesus Christ has not changed, from Saul on the road to Damascus to Tom Tarrants in Parchman State Prison in Mississippi. Each pursued his ends with a zeal that comes only with having a holy cause.

The holy cause of Saul we know. The holy cause of Tommy—white supremacy, total separation of the races, a battle against the Jewish conspiracy, and communism. Ridiculous? To you, maybe—to Tommy Tarrants, a cause he was willing to die for.

Political actions that most people doubt exist in this country were the daily bread of this young man. A rapid transition at age sixteen, starting innocently in the Goldwater campaign of 1964, and moving into the National States' Rights Party, the Ku Klux Klan, and the Minutemen—and briefly, a leader of Mississippi's dreaded White Knights of the KKK. Involved in planning and directing terrorist operations against civil rights forces, communists, liberals, and Jews, his daily tools were hand grenades, homemade bombs, pistols, and submachine guns. Fear was his greatest weapon. He would stop at nothing to attain his political goals.

Two bloody shootouts, a prison escape and recapture, years in maximum security and solitary confinement, tragedy after tragedy, and miracle after miracle were the mileposts of this young man's life. Tommy's story was a political fantasy—unbelievable in its savagery—until finally he found the transforming love of Jesus Christ. Tommy is now an intelligent, quiet, shy, and loving servant of the Lord.

I fought for my political beliefs as strongly as did Tommy—only through the system. We were political opposites. I was an advocate of much that he opposed. I'm convinced he would have killed me to accomplish his goals. Now Jesus Christ has made us brothers. We love one another. This is an amazing story of the love and the grace of our Lord.